DROP THE LEASH

Let Go of the Past and Love in the Present

Kathryn Eriksen

Miracle Income
Dallas, Texas

Drop the Leash: Let go of the Past and Love in the Present

By Kathryn Eriksen

ISBN: 978-0-9817283-6-0

DEDICATION

To love unconditionally, without reservation or judgment,

is life's highest calling.

To all dogs who lead with their hearts,

may you always find solace in a loving relationship.

And to the Human race,

may your heart surrender to love as willingly as your dog.

CONTENTS

INTRODUCTION

Dogs have always fascinated me. When you watch their behavior, especially around the people they love, it is like a dance. The dog sleeps until his human walks in the room, then the celebration begins. Whole body happiness, mixed with slobbering kisses and excited joy.

Watching my dogs repeat this dance of the heart over and over, it occurred to me to ask: "Why can't I live that way?"

I realized that I could be happy inside every moment, just like my dog. I just didn't know how.

So I decided to ask an expert. Avatar is the golden retriever that plays a key role in my novel, *Heart Dancing*, and he was the perfect character to share how dogs live in the moment.

That is how *Drop the Leash* was born.

Allow me to share a poem by Hafiz called "This Place Where You Are Right Now" that I hope will speak to your heart as it did mine.

This place where you are right now

God circled on a map for you.

Wherever your eyes and arms and heart can move

Against the earth and the sky,

The Beloved has bowed there –

Our Beloved has bowed there

Knowing You were coming.

You are here, sharing time and space with everyone on the planet, because **you have a purpose**. You are supposed to be right where you are, having experienced everything in your life that has brought you to this point.

That may sound "woo-woo" or unreal. It may be a lot to accept on blind faith. Until you open your eyes to the clues that are all around you.

Look into the eyes of your dog and tell me what you see.

Love, adoration and complete acceptance. Your dog reflects back what you already have inside of you. You have just forgotten.

This book was written to remind you of your divine essence. Your dog sees it clearly… but you may not see it because of old, limiting stories that are filtering your view of your life. When you begin to recognize those limiting stories and realize that they no longer serve you, that is the moment the door is open to growth, renewal and expansion.

Dogs know something that we have forgotten. When my dog looks at me, he sees a much better person than I believe I am.

I want to be the person my dog thinks I am. Don't you?

Even when I am angry or sad or depressed, my dog still sees me – the authentic me. I have spoken to many dog owners and they all share that common experience. Dogs *see us through the eyes of love, even when we don't see ourselves.*

You will quickly discover that this book is unlike any you have ever read. The content and lessons shared are from a dog's point of view. Avatar, the teacher and voice of the book, finally became so exasperated with the human race that he felt compelled to write this book. Think of it as an instruction manual from a dog who knows a thing or two about living inside every moment.

Thank you for sharing this incredible journey called Life. Life is meant to be lived wholeheartedly, joyously and together. Whenever you forget, just go spend some time with your dog.

Peace & Blessings,

Kathryn Eriksen

CHAPTER 1 - STOP ROLLING OVER AND PLAYING DEAD

I always see the light in you, even when you don't see it yourself. In those dark moments, look to me and I will remind you of your own light. – Avatar

It was a dark and stormy night. Rain poured down from the heavens in sheets, obscuring and redefining familiar shapes and objects. Water rushed down the street, creating torrents of flowing energy before spilling into the gutters like a raging waterfall.

A human shape slowly appeared, moving forward as her body separated the rain sheets with her hunched shoulders. She had given up trying to stay dry a long time ago. Her surrender to the elements was the outward response to her inner surrender to despair.

She moved purposefully and knew where to turn, reaching the makeshift shelter just as a ear-deafening clap of thunder shook the cardboard walls. She stooped down to move inside, grateful to have reached her home and get out of the rain.

The pounding of the water on the piece of tin that served as her roof was so loud that she missed the soft whining just outside her door. The girl rested with her eyes closed, breathing in the respite of her space. A sharp bark startled her back into the awareness of her situation.

She pulled back the old sheet that served as a shield against a harsh world, and saw a miserable looking dog, sitting patiently in the rain, mouth grinning in greeting, as if to say, "Finally!"

What she does next will determine the trajectory of her life. Will she allow her heart to open just a tiny bit to help another living being, or will she stay locked inside herself, dead to the world?

It's her choice to make. The consequences of her decision will set her on different paths, both of which end up at the same destination. The difference is what she experiences on the way.

This is my cue – when a human first opens the door and lets me in. This is where I go to work on a hardened heart to show the way back home. This is the work I was born to do. But I can't get started until you say "Yes, I am willing to change."

Willingness is different than persistence, perseverance or passion. Willingness is the starting point of these other attributes, the place where the first decision is made to shift. Willingness is elusive and easily forgotten in the mad rush of *doingness*. But it is the first step toward changing your life.

Are you willing to change your life?

The answer to that question will determine your next moment, hour, day, week, month and year. Your continued answer to that question as you move through space and time will set you on a path of inspiration and attunement. And the path back to yourself.

Are you willing to change your life?

Answer "Yes" and the door is open for the Universe to begin arranging people, situations and events to support your highest good. Say "No" to that question and the Universe still arranges people, situations and events to support your highest good. The difference is that **you** define your highest good with your answer. A "Yes" answer opens the door to infinite possibilities. A "No" keeps you locked into your current situation, clinging tightly to your pain, wrongs and fear.

Why am I sharing all of this with you?

Because that's my job – my reason to be here. I came to show you the way back home.

Who am I?

That's the question that we all want to answer, isn't it? Before you put this book down (or whatever the thing is that you are holding in your hand), let me explain a few things to you.

My name is Avatar and you might have guessed that I am a dog. Actually, I am so much more than a "dog" just as you are so much more than a "human," but for now, think of me as a dog.

No, that's not right either. Your concept of "dog" is a four-legged animal who only wants to eat, sleep and play. While that is true for many dogs you have lived with or encountered, it is only the beginning of how to describe me.

Physically, I inhabit the body of a golden retriever. Kind of large, with a big, goofy grin, I love to make people smile. When they run their hands (and especially their fingernails) down my back, I shiver. I know when my master is sad or grumpy and I know how to make her smile. She and I have traveled some rough roads together but we are both at the place where we share and teach what we know to be true.

Her name is Avery and her lessons can be found in a book called *Heart Dancing: A Story Alchemy Adventure (by Kathryn Eriksen)*.

This is my book. The lessons taught within are based on many observations of the differences between humans and dogs. It has always made me wonder why humans make things so complicated, when life is really very simple.

Eat. Play. Sleep. Repeat.

That's it. That is the fabric of this experience called "life."

Are you buying that? If so, then you might as well put down this book and go back to your dull, boring life. Those are the physical needs that both humans and dogs share.

I want to focus on the spiritual – the Divine essence inside all living things. The energy that runs like a golden thread through the plants, animals and humans sharing this blue, spinning globe called Earth.

Why is a dog sharing this with you?

What Dogs Know that You Ignore

Anyone who has ever lived with a dog and watched them closely knows that dogs are unique among animals. Your dog is a member of your family, treasured for his company and valued for his presence. Sometimes, people mourn the loss of their dog more deeply sometimes than their human companions.

I know why that happens. It all comes down to relationship. Your relationship with your dog is simple, pure adoration and admiration. There is no judgment or criticism – only a mutual respect and love.

> **A love affair between a human and a dog is a wondrous thing to behold. A love affair between two humans...not so much.**

Humans tend to complicate the communication and the purpose of relationships. Unspoken needs, unfulfilled desires and unseen fears operate beneath the surface and can cause a tsunami of gigantic proportions. Most people never see it coming. They think that they are discussing one topic, when they are really communicating on another, unseen level.

When the intent, motivation and purpose underlying the communication is not in alignment with the spoken words, that is the moment that misunderstandings, hurt feelings and anger disrupt the flow of meaning. The tsunami of energy causes an earthquake in the relationship and deep fissures or chasms can result.

All because humans ignore what dogs know.

Dogs keep it simple. We know why we are here, next to you, patiently waiting for you to hug or pet us. We know what we are doing when we lean against you, offering comfort and support. We understand the power of silence and have a huge capacity for giving. Dogs listen much better than most humans (and it has nothing to do with our superior hearing).

Dogs are here to love with all of their body, mind and heart. Humans are too, but you ignore that truth. I am not being judgmental, because I know that you know that you are here to love and be loved.

I don't pretend to understand humans or why you make yourselves so miserable. That is certainly your choice. But why choose the hard way when there is a much easier way *to be* in the world?

I am here to remind you.

Are Humans and Dogs So Different?

I have pondered this question and have finally found the answer. Humans and dogs are really not so different; humans just *think* they are. If humans only took their cues on how to act from their dog, the world would look much different.

Here is an example of the way humans complicate the simple needs of a good life. Have you ever heard of Maslow's Hierarchy of Needs? The most basic of challenges for humans is to satisfy their physical needs. After those are met, safety needs are next. Only when humans feel safe (according to Maslow) can they seek love and belonging. Esteem and self-actualization are the highest level of needs.

Many happiness experts base their practices on Maslow's Hierarchy of Needs, which is shown in the following diagram. The only problem is that the highest level is not achievable until the lower level of needs have been met. It is truly a step-by-step process of moving upward through each level.

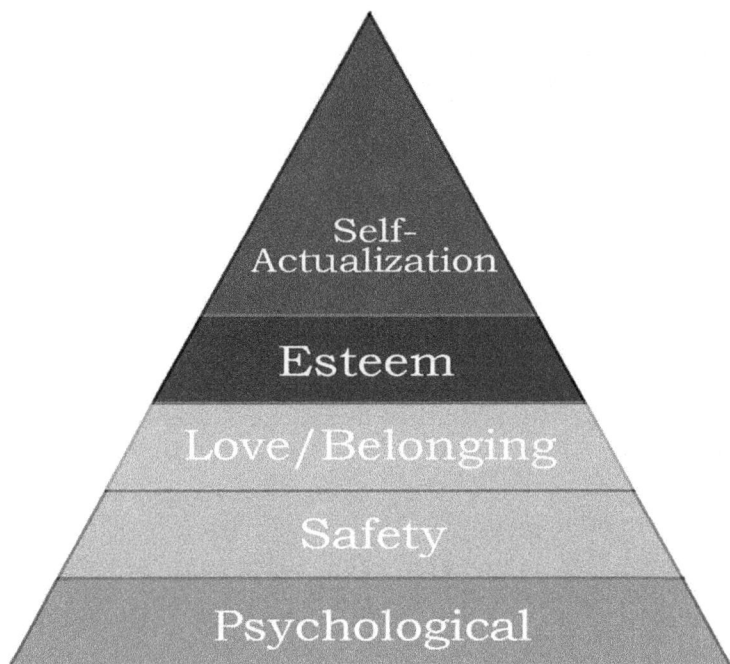

According to Maslow, the most fundamental needs must be

satisfied before a human can achieve any success in the higher levels. It is a stair-step process of moving from one level to the next.

That may have been fine for Maslow, but there is another way to achieve happiness.

Dogs approach life from a completely different perspective. The starting point for dogs is: *whatever gives freedom to live in the moment, enjoy the ride and love with all of our hearts (and bodies).*

Don't believe me? Just watch the next dog you see hanging his head out of the window of that metal thing that moves. I can guarantee that you have never seen such an expression of bliss, happiness and love on any one face, as on the face of that dog. He is totally in the moment, drinking in all of the smells that rush by him without him having to do a thing. Except enjoy the ride.

Dogs know how to live in the moment. Humans, not so much.

And that my friends, is the key to happiness. **To be fully present in this moment, without a thought of the past or future.**

That dog you see hanging his head out the window is not thinking about the squirrel he chased out of his yard earlier that morning. He is not thinking about his next meal or where his human is taking him. In fact, *he is not thinking at all.* He is fully alive, in that moment, experiencing everything that is rushing by him. Without judgment, doubt or anxiety.

Give yourself permission to allow this moment to be exactly as it is and allow yourself to be exactly as you are. Take a deep breath and just let those words settle in. You might even repeat after me:

**I give myself permission to allow this moment to be
exactly as it is and to allow myself to be exactly as I am.**

In this moment.

Doesn't that feel better – to stop the constant stream of thoughts in your head and just *be* present? Did you feel the stress or tension in your body loosen just a bit? Do you feel calmer and more aware of yourself and your physical world?

You have just tasted a moment of bliss. The same bliss that dogs experience, naturally, easily and effortlessly. You can learn to be present in every moment, but it will take looking at your world through a different set of lenses.

Please sit patiently, while I present another way to live. I promise you it will be worth the wait.

Doglow's Hierarchy of Connection

Maslow was on to something, but I am here to show you a different hierarchy, the one that describe how dogs live their lives. It was created by a brilliant canine named Doglow. Before you roll your eyes (or you already may have done so), please give me a moment to explain this new way of living.

May I present Doglow's Hierarchy of Connection, which demonstrates how dogs live in the world.

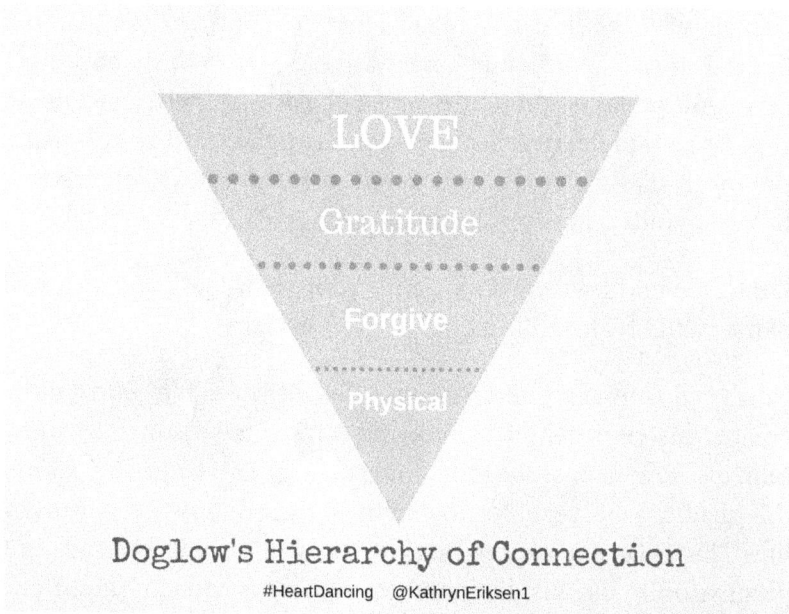

Doglow's Hierarchy of Connection

#HeartDancing   @KathrynEriksen1

I am sure that you noticed that Doglow's pyramid is upside down – inverted. That's because physical needs are the smallest and easiest to satisfy. As we move higher up the pyramid, the capacity (and consciousness) to become open to the next level increases.

Notice the difference in the lines that separate the levels in Maslow's pyramid. They are solid and almost look like barriers, blocking each level from the other. Doglow knew that connection happens on all levels, and he deliberately created his pyramid with space between each level. The connection between each level is also shown by sharing the same color, instead of different colors.

You may be wondering why forgiveness is the next level of connection after physical needs are met. This book is my explanation as to **why you must forgive first**. Forgiveness opens the heart to gratitude and love. **Without forgiveness, you remain locked in your story of being wronged, slighted or rejected.**

That is why this book is called *Drop the Leash*. As long as you believe stories about your past that hold you back or no longer serve you, you are tied to the same behavior and will continue to repeat the same patterns. When you drop the leash by following the forgiveness formula and exercises in this book, you are free to live joyfully...in the present moment.

Gratitude and love will flood into your awareness and you will dance with life. Just like a dog. Go figure, right?

I do need to make one disclaimer before we move on. Doglow created his Hierarchy of Connection for one reason – to show humans how to live more like dogs. Dogs don't need to follow this diagram because we instinctively know how to approach life. This is a wink from Doglow himself to you. He gave me permission to use his diagram because this is such an important concept and crucial to your happiness.

Back to Doglow's pyramid. After physical needs are met, forgiveness opens the way for gratitude and love to flood into your awareness.

First – *Forgive* >

Second – *Be Grateful* >

Third and Always – *Love*

This will be the road map on our journey together.

"What journey?"

Of course you focused on that part of my statement, instead of where we will go. Ugh, humans can be so...human. You will soon learn that I have little patience for shallow thinking, lazy thoughts or plain dullness.

There are three stages of this journey, but in reality, they all occur at once. For the sake of your understanding, I have bundled the concepts into three seemingly distinct parts. Forgiveness will be shared in this book. The next book will focus on gratitude and love, really two sides of the same coin.

But wait – I am getting ahead of myself.

Life is a journey of discovery. You are an explorer, a daring adventurer who wants to experience, feel and connect with all that life has to offer.

Are you ready to begin?

The Journey

My name is Avatar and I am a Master Teacher. "Teacher of what?" you might ask. (There you go again, focusing on the easy word and not the more difficult concept). For now, just accept that I am a Master Teacher, because I have seen, lived through and learned about life in ways you will never know or understand.

I was sent here to be your guide – your seeing eye dog – if you will let me.

You may not realize that you are blind to the beauty of life that surrounds you in every moment. You are oblivious to the loving energy that connects all living creatures. There is a simple reason why you don't know about the loving energy – because no one ever taught it to you.

That is my ultimate goal with this material – to demonstrate once and for all that we all come from the same Source. And that makes all the difference in how you see your world. It also allows forgiveness to flow freely so you can enjoy the upper levels of Doglow's Connections.

I was sent to be your seeing eye dog – your guide back to your Self. Just as a blind person develops a relationship with her dog and comes to depend on the dog's superior eyesight, hearing and smell, you can do the same with me.

But instead of guiding you through the physical world, I will guide you through the spiritual.

Remember the story I told you in the beginning? The homeless girl who is totally defeated and about to give up hope, when she hears a noise outside of her shelter? Why did I tell you that story?

Because at some point in your life, you have been homeless. You drifted and shifted on the whims of the wind. Like a leaf that floats and swirls in the autumn breeze, you never felt as if you had a place…or a choice.

Is that how you feel right now? No direction, no connection, no choices? Or you may believe that because of your past decisions, you have no future. Perhaps you think that you are not entitled to happiness. Or love.

It's perfectly O.K. to feel that way, as long as you don't *believe* you are that way. That's the tricky thing about emotions – they are there to let you know the state of your *being*. The trouble starts when you identify with the emotion and think-you-are-that.

I can see the dazed look on your face. Sorry about that, I jumped ahead of myself.

We are going on a journey together. By the end of this book, you will discover that you are in a different place than when we started. You will also be in a different relationship with your physical world, your human connections and most importantly, with your Self.

Of course, this journey never ends. After you integrate the knowledge and information I share, other teachers will come across your path. You may choose to listen and follow their advice, or you can decide to listen within, to your own GPS (God Positioning Software).

You came to this time and place with a built-in GPS, did you know that?

Silence…crickets chirping. Sigh…I can see that I have to go back to the beginning of the story – our story together.

Before you ask any more questions, just sit back, take a moment to close your eyes and breathe deeply 3 times, then come back to these words.

Are you back now? Good, then let's begin again.

When humans first walked the earth, they only focused on surviving from one moment to the next. Finding food and shelter took all their time and energy. The higher needs of connection, purpose and love were not even contemplated, much less pursued.

One night, sitting around the fire they had recently learned to create, the flickering light danced with the dark. The humans took in the moment and smiled, knowing that at least for now, they were safe. They huddled closer to the warm flames and listened to the night sounds around them.

Suddenly, there was a faint sound of twigs snapping. The man jumped to his feet, grasping his only weapon, ready to defend his family. He stared into the night, trying to see through the darkness and identify the threat before it charged him.

As he stood there in warrior pose, the woman peeked around him and noticed two small eyes staring back at her, close to the ground. She moved closer to see what it was and then she heard it. A soft whimpering that went straight to her heart.

It slowly crawled from the darkness into the glow of the light. Dragging itself on the ground, its posture one of total submission, the whimpering began again as the animal looked up with pleading eyes.

The man released his breath and sighed. His body relaxed and he returned to his seat at the campfire, grateful that the threat was not serious.

The woman was captivated with the creature. It was just a baby, shivering and cold. She gently picked it up and settled it in her lap. The furry animal was startled at first, but soon settled into the warmth of her body and fell sound asleep.

From that day on, dogs have submitted their freedom to humans in exchange for their love. Humans have opened their hearts to dogs... in exchange for love.

A beautiful, dynamic relationship was born out of necessity and grew out of shared needs. A silent pact was made that still exists today. Dogs give their love openly and freely, while humans give them shelter, companionship and friendship.

Some humans go much deeper and see the light of something greater shining from a dog's eyes. And for a lucky few, when they see the light of something greater in the dog's eyes, they also see it reflected back to them in their own eyes.

They realize that dogs know more about life and how to live it than most humans.

And so it is.

That is the story of the first dog/human connection. That story is told to every dog ever born, so even as a puppy, every dog knows his purpose and goal while he is in dog-form:

- To love at least one human, completely, unconditionally and without holding back.
- And to show a human *how to* love completely, without holding back.

This was the plan from the beginning of time – for dogs to act as reminders of something greater, something bigger than what the five senses can experience. And for the most part, it has worked. Dogs are beloved around the world for their loyalty, friendship, and ability to listen without judgment.

But it isn't enough.

Why this book?

I was called to write this book and share this knowledge with you for one reason – it's time for you to move up to the next level in Doglow's Hierarchy of Connection. The world (i.e., humans) is stuck at the bottom level of taking care of physical needs. Despite every effort by every dog on the planet to demonstrate the higher levels, people just don't get it. They aren't paying attention.

Consider this book a wake-up call to **STOP ROLLING OVER AND PLAYING DEAD.**

Sorry, I get a little carried away with the urgency of what faces us. There is a shift in the energy around you. I know you can feel it. The weather patterns are different – more severe and out of sync with normal seasons. Natural disasters occur much more frequently than ever before and impacts people all over the globe. Ecosystems are dying, some from man's behavior (the Amazon Rain Forest comes to mind) and others, like the Great Barrier Reef, from unexplained natural changes.

And it's not just our physical environment that is waving the red flag that things need to change. It is also in human relationships – how you interact and relate to each other. From countries who close their borders to refugees, to people of different skin color behaving as if *they* are the only humans...

I could go on naming all of the big problems that we face. But I am most interested in your relationship with yourself. Why? Because the problems we see in the physical world stem from the chaos that is inside. The outer world is merely a reflection of the inner world.

When your inner world is calm, you see differently, speak more thoughtfully and act with integrity. And those ripples will shift the outer world, especially your relationships to other people and how you show up in every moment. When you begin to understand that *first you go within before you think, speak or act,* that is the pivot point that will change your life.

My goal is to introduce you — to Your Self. You probably haven't spent much time with Your Self lately, but that's O.K. Your Self is patiently waiting for you to be still and listen. Your Self never judges or criticizes. It is unconditional love, waiting to meet you. It is deep, infinite and eternal. And it can only be touched in the space of gratitude and love.

Dogs live from the space of gratitude and love. It's who we are. Humans can also live from the same space, but you complicate your life *by telling stories about your experience, instead of being the experience.* It is precisely that ability to assign meaning to events, people and relationships that humans have to forgive before they can live in gratitude and love.

I know what I just said probably caused a scrunched up look on your face. You may have even scratched or cocked your head to the side. I promise it will all become clearer as we move forward.

It's time for a quiz. Can you answer "Yes!" to each of these questions:

- Do you allow yourself time to simply be here, right now?
- Do you have value despite what the world says about you?
- Are you in love with yourself?

If you said "Yes!" after reading each question, then kudos! You can stop reading and I will refund your money :-). For all of you who hesitated or said "No" to any of these questions, I can help.

Remember, I am your seeing eye dog on this journey together. As you move through and adopt forgiveness, you will be ready for the next level – Gratitude. Gratitude naturally leads to the final connection – love. And unconditional love makes forgiveness doable.

Instead of Doglow's Hierarchy of Connection, I like to explain it this way: **When you forgive your past, you see your present moment more clearly.** Gratitude is a natural response and brings the gift of clarity to what is in front of you, which opens the door to connection with a higher power – love.

Remember, you are constantly moving energy as you experience these different states. The energies of forgiveness, gratitude and love are all made of the same frequency. They are just different expressions of the same thing — Love.

Dogs live inside this cycle of love and don't need to forgive. Humans forget to live from this cycle and think, speak and act from their egos, not their hearts. Ego-speak creates separation; Love-speak is unity.

Forgive → Gratitude → Love

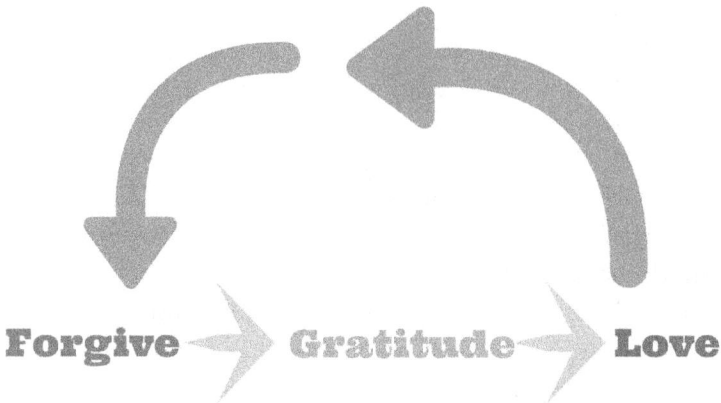

It's a never ending cycle of
energy
that continually
flows, expands and gives.

It all starts with forgiveness.

#HeartDancing   @KathrynEriksen1

This continuously flowing energy is always there, available to every being on the planet. Animals and plants connect to it without thought; humans fall into the trap of believing their thoughts, which blocks their connection to this cycle. Animals know how to live from this place; humans must remember it.

Forgiveness is the entry point to the never ending cycle of love.

When you learn to forgive your past, your mistakes and your doubt about your value, you step into a new energy. Think of it as a dance and your partner is Life. As you reconnect with Life and drop the leash of your limiting stories, you step into living in the present moment. Other people's opinions about you don't matter, because you know you are valued and loved. Or else you would never be here.

You are meant to be the most authentic expression of you. You are here for a specific purpose that only you can fill. And it's up to you to forgive your stories, forgive yourself and others, and step into your own magnificence.

Dogs really don't forgive because we never step out of the loop. Dogs are constantly aligned inside the cycle. **To a dog, life looks like this diagram:**

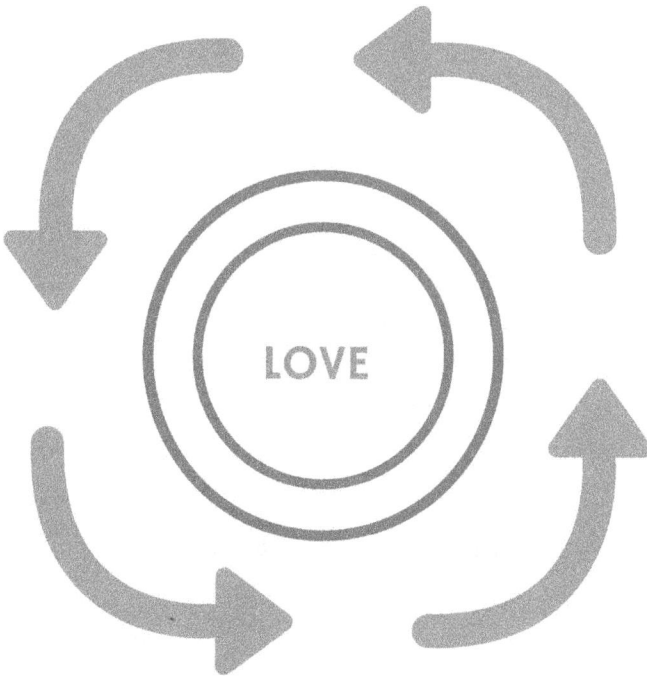

LOVE

#HeartDancing   @KathrynEriksen1

The cycle of love is how we are designed to live our lives. When you were a baby, you were completely planted inside the inner circle of unconditional love. You never left that inner circle and your energy flowed from you, infused with love.

So what happens as the baby grows up? That is one of the questions I answer as we move down the path together. By the end, you will understand your role in the cycle of life and how you can improve your awareness of your own magnificence.

Yes – I am pointing my paw at you. Sit up a little straighter please. It's time for you – yes, YOU – to step up into the next level of Connection. That is what I am going to teach you – the how and why of the higher level…of forgiveness.

As seen through the eyes of a dog.

The Class Syllabus

Pretend that we are at the start of the semester and you have just met me. While you are sizing me up, I hand out a syllabus (excuse the paw prints). It gives you an overview of the topics and the order that they will be presented:

- **Who is Holding Your Leash?**
  A Dog's Definition of Forgiveness
  A Human's Definition of Forgiveness
  Release and Let Go
  Only Humans Create Stories

- **Stop Chasing Your Tail (Tale)**
  You See with Your Mind, Not Your Eyes
  Why is this so Important?
  Forgiveness Leads to *Beingness*

- **Paws and Heel (Pause and Heal)**
  Forgiveness Steps
  Recognize your Fear Stories
  Realize you Created Them
  Responsibility

Reframe & Release

- **Bury the Bone**
    3 Types of Forgiveness
    Never Forget the Kong
    Listen in Silence
    What's Next?

Hopefully, by now you have set aside all doubts and concerns about learning from a d-o-g. I know how to live from my heart, not my head…you could learn a thing or two about that!

Before we dive into the material, just know that I received special dispensation from the Dog Council to share this information with you. What I am about to teach you has been highly classified ever since dogs first set foot on the earth. *Way before* that first pup showed up at the caveman's campfire.

Ever wonder *why* that first pup stepped out of the darkness into the light made by man?

Think of it from our perspective. Here we are, roaming the earth having a fine time, making our own rules and living in our own society, when we are asked to help out a human.

What???? With that startled expression still on your face (I do love to do that to you :-)), let's begin.

CHAPTER 2 - WHO IS HOLDING YOUR LEASH?

Dogs don't need to forgive. People do. – Avatar

When you walk your dog, you have a physical connection with him. The leash is attached to his collar or harness and you are at the other end, holding on and perhaps directing the walk.

Humans don't live with leashes around their necks. Instead, they place a leash on their minds. Habitual thinking about past events erupt in the present moment, coloring what is happening now. People who trigger your past stories are cautiously regarded and the communication (through words and energy) becomes murky with hidden meanings. When you decide that you were *this way* (that you were clumsy, stupid, impulsive, not worthy – the list goes on and on) about a past event, it will continue to act as a filter when a similar circumstance presents itself.

Are you starting to catch a glimmer of who is holding your leash?

Learning to drop the leash and step into your authenticity, vibrancy and brilliance is why I wrote this book. Guess what the first concept is on the journey of dropping your leash?

Forgiveness.

Forgiveness is an elusive concept that can morph in meaning, depending on who is talking. To one person, it might mean being the bigger person and letting the other poor slob off the hook. To another, forgiveness means that they are the better person because they "forgave."

It always best to remember that when you forgive, it isn't because the other person deserves it. Forgiveness releases you from the past so you can allow the present to flow into a larger, grander future. When you don't forgive, you remain anchored to that painful event and miss all of the beauty and grandeur of the present moment.

It's almost as if your life is a waterfall of clear water. As you move through time and space, you can allow the energy to flow freely through you. Or you can become attached to a painful memory and use it to filter the flow. Instead of being fully present, *in this moment*, your past acts like a sieve, filtering out anything that doesn't match the memory. And the waterfall of energy is diverted, altered and reshaped to match your filter.

Humans have been called "meaning making machines." When something happens, a human will create a story about that event. A story is the *meaning* humans give to a situation, person or circumstance about *what it means to them*. That individual story then becomes the filter for the next moment.

Dogs don't create stories. Dog simply live in this moment, then in this moment, over and over.

It's important to note that dogs really don't "forgive" as we have been discussing. Dogs do their thing – love unconditionally – so they don't need to forgive. *Because to a dog, there is nothing to forgive. To a human, everything is a call for forgiveness.*

Dogs stepped into the light of the campfire all those centuries ago to remind humans of a grander vision of life. We know how to live in bliss, happiness and joy. Humans have forgotten, but with our help, you can remember and join us in the Heart Dance.

A Dog's Definition of Forgiveness

Before I share a dog's definition of forgiveness, let me explain why I sometimes use the slanted writing you call *italics*. It is a visual cue for you to sit and think about the message. Write it down in your journal or in your phone; consider how it might look in your daily life if you accepted it as truth and allowed it to guide your thoughts, beliefs and actions. Chew on it like it was a dog bone:-)

If a dog could talk, he would define forgiveness in these words:

Forgiveness is seeing the light of love in the other person, no matter what they did.

Think about your dog. Have you ever accidentally stepped on his foot (or tail)? A quick yelp might be the instant response, but then that mutt is all over you, wanting you to know that it's O.K.

That is forgiveness, pure and simple. No judgment, no criticism, no self-righteousness.

Just pure, simple love.

So I know you are wondering about a more severe situation, when a dog is deliberately hurt or abused. Do those people deserve forgiveness?

One of the cardinal rules that all dogs live by is:

People sometimes don't know what they do or why they are doing it. We love them anyway.

A dog's job on earth is to love. That's it. And when you come from a place of love, there is no judgment. Love covers it, absorbs the pain and releases the hurt. That is why forgiveness comes so easily to a dog.

On a practical note, should the dog stay with someone who continues to abuse them? No, absolutely not! The abuser is not acting from a loving place and no dog (or human) should tolerate that. Will the dog still forgive the abuser? Yes – without hesitation. Because a dog's number one priority is to love, no matter what.

Sometimes the light of forgiveness can penetrate the darkness inside the human. Sometimes, it can't. Dogs don't have control over what happens to the love light they send. Their job is to send it anyway.

Forgiveness has nothing to do with the other person and everything to do with you. Dogs understand this fundamental principle. But people just can't seem to grasp such a simple concept.

Let's see how well you do…

A Human's Definition of Forgiveness

Somehow, somewhere, people adopted the idea that they are the bigger and better person when they forgive another for hurting them. It's like the forgiver feels so good about stepping up, they place themselves on the Forgiveness Pedestal so everyone can see just how good a person they are!

Have you ever done that? "Forgiven" so you could be applauded? How did that feel after you announced your "forgiveness" – were you at peace in the situation? Or did you pay close attention to the other people involved to make sure they knew how big a sacrifice you were making?

I have seen many people in all kinds of situations. I have observed their brand of "forgiveness" and I have come to call it "fake forgiveness." It really isn't forgiveness – it is more like an act to shine a spotlight on you, instead of you shining your light of love on the person.

See the difference?

When the intention behind "fake forgiveness" is to pat yourself on the back, it isn't forgiveness. That is just a label, not the real deal. There is still subtle judgment of the other person and a sense that they should be happy that you (there's that spotlight again) are so great.

The best way to describe the energy flow is to show you:

Fake Forgiveness

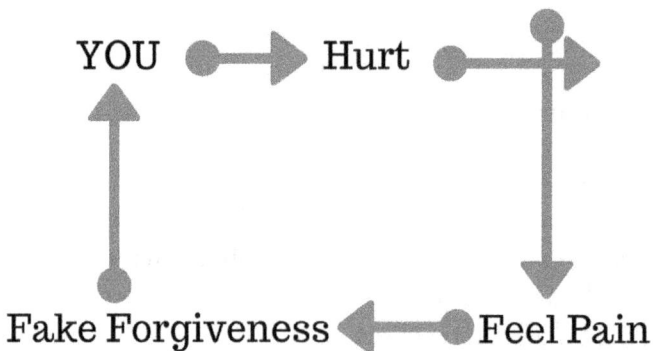

YOU ●→ Hurt ●→●

Fake Forgiveness ←● Feel Pain

No one is healed.
Only your ego is appeased.

#HeartDancing   @KathrynEriksen1

Notice how the energy spins around on itself? It starts with You and it ends with You. It is a closed loop – a closed circuit that doesn't allow anything else in. It also demands certain responses from the other person – the forgivee. If that person doesn't accept the fake forgiveness you so generously offer, then the entire cycle starts again, with you being hurt, etc.

You know when forgiveness is fake. So does the other person. So why are you surprised when they don't accept your generous forgiveness?

The problem with fake forgiveness is two-fold:

- It makes you feel as though you are in the right, because only you, the forgiver, can forgive the other person; and
- It does nothing to heal the situation; instead, it creates another layer of friction.

Remember the dog's view of forgiveness – it has nothing to do with the other person and everything to do with you.

To forgive like a dog, first you must *know that you have the light of love inside of you*. You came from love and you will return to love. This is the basic point of knowledge from which all else springs. It is also the pivot point between dogs and people.

Dogs get it. People don't.

Why? I have pondered that question for many years and I think I have an answer. Dogs and humans start out at the same place before they come to earth. The same loving energy that created everything we see also created dogs and humans.

This can't be proven under a microscope, but it also can't be *disproved either*.

It is a choice that is made by every human that ever took their first breath. Dogs never have the choice to make, because they are gifted with the *knowledge of love*.

And that, my friend is the difference between dogs and people.

Dogs have no choice but to love unconditionally. Humans have the freedom to choose between love or fear in every moment and each tick of the clock.

The freedom to choose is a blessing and a curse.

When you love unconditionally, forgiveness is just like breathing. The bigger love that you allow into your heart pours out of you in the form of forgiveness. Nothing blocks the flow as it is expressed by you.

The energy flow of Forgiveness looks like this:

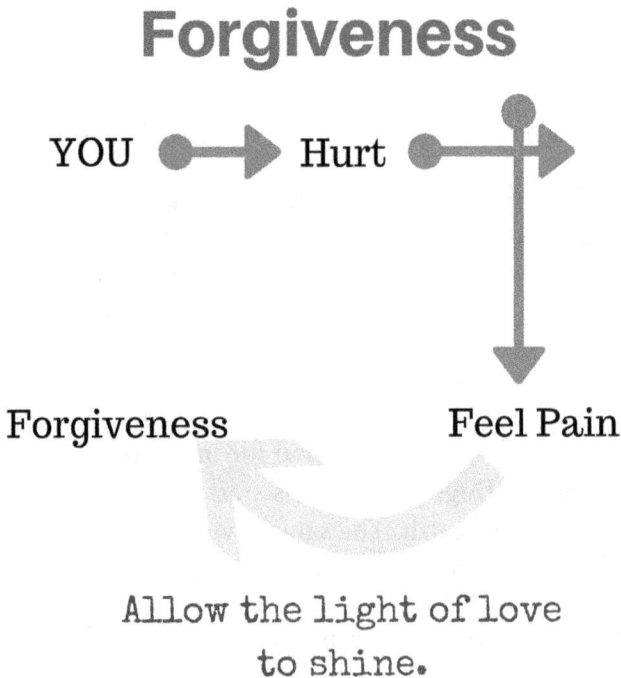

Forgiveness

YOU → Hurt →

Forgiveness   Feel Pain

Allow the light of love
to shine.

#HeartDancing   @KathrynEriksen1

This is an open loop that allows for something bigger to enter the picture. Call it what you will, but when you ask for help because you know you are not strong enough, mature enough or willing enough, it completely changes the equation.

What is being added to the mix? Unconditional love.

Dogs don't have to ask for unconditional love. Dogs are unconditional love.

People are also unconditional love, but they don't believe it. They are given the choice to believe it or not inside every moment of every day. When they choose not to believe that they came from love and they are that love, that's when things can get a bit dicey.

I am here to remind you that you and I are made from the same stuff. We came from the same place and we will return to that place. That's why it's O.K. to acknowledge that you don't know it all, you can never control the outcome and you are at a loss as to what to do next.

That is the time to ask for help.

When you don't ask for help, you communicate that you think you can do it all. Fake forgiveness isn't too far behind that train of thinking. Look closely where that takes you. Not to any place where there is clarity, peace, joy and love. That train will always drop you off at the depot of despair, desperation and depression.

Fake forgiveness also separates you from yourself and others. When you are tied up in your story of being right, you are isolated from any other viewpoint of possibility. It's a zero sum game, because you think you hold all of the cards.

Let's compare the consequences of fake forgiveness versus real forgiveness:

Fake Forgiveness	Real Forgiveness
The hurt never heals;	The hurt always heals;
Your expectations are never met;	There are no expectations to be fulfilled by the other person.
You are justified in your position and don't see what you did to contribute to the situation;	Right or wrong doesn't matter in the light of love.
Both people stay stuck. Neither grows.	You grow from the experience.
You remain the victim and never find peace.	You reclaim your power and find peace.

#HeartDancing   @KathrynEriksen1

Fake forgiveness is all about you – it circles back on itself. It never releases the hurt or upset; it only ties it up with a big bow so you can pull it out to show your friends.

Which brings up another consequence of fake forgiveness. When you practice fake forgiveness for any length of time, you may discover that you have lost your true friends. No one wants to spend their time with someone who only focuses on themselves and their needs. No amount of pleading or passionate argument will change the lack of sincerity. It comes all from the head, not the heart. People can spot that a mile away.

Real forgiveness is also about you, but it springs from a yearning to learn from this experience, grow and expand into something bigger. It comes from a heartfelt desire to heal as quickly as possible. And the only way to do that is to release and let go.

Release and Let Go

Are you catching a glimpse of how dogs forgive? Watch your dog the next time you move your chair and accidentally nip his tail. He will express his hurt, but then start licking you or his tail will say, "Sorry about that. You startled me and it hurt just a bit, but now I am back to loving you."

Dogs do get hurt. Their feelings get hurt when you ignore them or yell at them (even though they may deserve it!). Here's another Dog Bone to remember:

> *Dogs never hold on to the hurt for very long. Instead, dogs release and let go.*

Can you say the same thing for humans? How many centuries have some tribes or cultures held onto a past grievance or misunderstanding? How many times have you repeated the same, sad story of hurt, abuse and betrayal to anyone who would listen with a sympathetic ear (your dog, for example)?

During one of my lifetimes, I was a hunting dog. My master took me to a place that was really cold, but it had a rushing river so I got to play in the water. One day, he fired that long stick and a bird fell out of the sky! He told me to go find it and bring it back to him, which I did very quickly (dead birds have a particularly strong smell).

When I brought the bird back to him, he asked me to "drop it." I didn't want to, because all of my instincts were saying, "No – I found the bird. I should be able to keep it!" My master knew I was still very new to the hunting concept, so he patiently asked me to "drop it" but in a sterner voice. His tone finally reached the level that I knew I had better obey or something would happen to me that I wouldn't like.

So, without a lot of drama, I dropped the stupid bird.

You would have thought I did some fantastic thing by the way he acted. He gushed; he praised me; he claimed to the heavens that I was the best hunting dog on the face of the planet (that one did make me grin and got my tail wagging). On that day, I learned to drop and release birds.

Of course, with forgiveness I already knew to drop and release. For dogs, it comes naturally. For people, it is a learned skill.

Why is it so important to "release and let go" when you are forgiving someone?

You have to be *willing* to release the hurt, pain and anger you feel toward the other person and the situation before you can move into the space of forgiveness. It is your *attachment* to the hurt, pain and anger that keeps your heart locked up and your ability to forgive frozen. When you are still attached to your feelings, it is much more difficult to forgive.

Imagine that you are eating lunch in a crowded restaurant with a friend, when a stranger bumps your table and your phone is knocked to the concrete floor. Before you can do anything, someone else steps on it.

This happens in less than 2 seconds, but the anger you feel at being an "innocent victim" stays with you. The person who stepped on your phone refused to pay for the damage – he didn't know it was on the floor. The other guy who knocked it over was also belligerent and refused to take responsibility.

What are you supposed to do – forgive and forget? How could that ever happen?

Instead of "forgive and forget" (that makes it sound so passive), think of it as "release and let go." For you to release your anger, you have to be in control of it. To be in control of your anger means that you are bigger than your emotions. To be bigger than your emotions means that you can choose a different emotion.

Release the anger and replace it with peace.

Release and let go still allows you time to feel your anger, but when it has run its course, you decide to release your strong emotions against those strangers. Letting go helps you clear up your own energy and you are no longer tied to the other person.

When you don't release and let go, it's like you are pointing an accusatory finger at the other person and completely ignoring the 4 fingers pointing back at you. It's the poison *you drink* that you want to harm the other person involved, but *it only harms you.*

Why in the world would you want to keep hurting yourself by your anger? What possible reason could there be to hold onto your hurt when you know that it keeps you upset, agitated and anxious? This is one of the sides of human behavior that I obviously do not understand, so forgive my ranting.

After all of my lifetimes observing people, after living with many different types of humans, I have come to the only conclusion that makes sense. It's one of the main differences between dogs and people and it always keeps people stuck. It is true across cultures, civilizations, countries and across all of the years that humans and dogs have walked the earth.

Dogs don't need to be right. They just love.

People need to be right. They choose being right instead of love.

The need to be right is what prevents you from reaching for forgiveness. Let's go back to the cell phone example. When your phone was destroyed by other people, you felt that they should pay for it. Even though on the surface you were "right," at some point you recognized that you couldn't force the other people to accept that you were "right." You face a decision that is the crux of whether you remain in your victim story or move on past the incident. The decision is whether you take action to prove you are "right" or do you drop it and regain peace.

If you chose to pursue it and the final result was that your phone was paid for by one or both of the other people, did that make you feel better? Was peace your final goal or was it to satisfy the need to be right?

What if you had chosen to release and let go? When you recognized that your need to be right was creating more turmoil than necessary, you could have stepped back from the situation and asked yourself these questions:

- What am I feeling right now? Is it based on fear or love?
- If I am feeling an emotion based on fear, why am I afraid?
- Is my fear based in the past or the future?
- What if I chose to love in this situation?

Moving through your fear into love is what you came to learn because of this experience. You may not see that now or agree with it. That's O.K. You may not be ready or you may forget. Your dog will always remind you that there is a better way.

Dogs turn away from their hurt back to love in an instant. Humans, not so fast. Dogs know that they are love and that love is their natural emotional state.

Humans knew this truth when they were babies. Does a baby hold onto anger or frustration after her bodily needs are met? Of course not – because a baby knows she came from love and she is love. Love is her natural state. She has no choice but to return to love, because she doesn't judge herself or others (she hasn't learned that skill yet).

When you think about it, a baby and a dog are a lot alike. Neither one has a need to be right. Neither one judges or holds onto any other emotion except love. And neither one forgets who they are.

What creates the separation from Self that humans struggle with so desperately? Why is a two-year-old child so different from a baby (or a dog, for that matter)? What happens between the time a child is born and the first time that same child doesn't automatically forgive?

One word – language.

Actually, it more than one word (pun intended). Language is the gift that humans received and dogs didn't. The ability to communicate with words, symbols and signs is what sets apart people from every other creature on the planet.

But language is a gift and a curse.

The ability to speak words and communicate can be breathtaking, inspiring, motivating and uplifting. The creation of expression is artistry in itself. (I have to admit; I am enjoying this freedom to use words to paint pictures or illustrate a point).

We will explore the impact of language on forgiveness in the next section. For now, I will remind you to release and let go. Following the need to be right is just like when I follow a bunny trail and discover that it is a dead end. It's a trick to make you think something is there, so you spend a lot of time and energy trying to find it. But in the end, you have nothing. Nada. Zip. Zero.

Learn to release and let go. Follow your dog's lead and remember one of the first Dog Bones you learned. (or we could call it *dogma* – lol).

> *Forgiveness is seeing the light of love in the other person, no matter what they did.*

Dogs are always connected to Divine love. Dogs *are* Divine love. You are too – you just forgot in the sandstorm of your emotions. When you become attached to your emotions and enjoy *being that feeling*, true forgiveness is impossible.

How do you make the shift from being the emotion to forgiveness? You act like a dog and drop it.

Dogs do not hold onto any emotion…except love. Remember the last time you hurt your dog's feelings? You knew you did because of that look in your pup's eyes of hurt, betrayal or rejection. (if you have read this far into this book, then you are a dog person so I really don't have to explain myself).

How long did that hurt look last? A second or two? And did you notice that just behind the hurt look was the look of the continuous beat of love?

As soon as you apologized to your dog – what was his reaction? Did he hold onto his hurt and refuse to accept your apology? I can guarantee you that he jumped into your arms or danced around at your feet and told you in every way he possibly could that "It's O.K. I know you didn't mean it. Can we go outside and play now?"

The next time you find yourself wallowing in your justified emotions, think of your dog. Then go out and play.

Only Humans Create Stories

Remember what I said about language being a blessing and a curse? Here is where we get deeper into that subject.

When dogs are born, they learn very quickly how to find their mother (the source of all things good) and they decipher the pecking order in the pack. Larger beats smaller, persistence usually pays off and it's always best to mind your mama. Communication is accomplished through physical touching (nudging, licking, etc.), body language (ears alert or down, gaze fixed, etc.) and audible sounds (whining, barking, etc.). The spectrum of canine communication is absorbed by the first 10 weeks of life.

Human babies take a bit longer to acclimatize to their new physical environment. An infant learns very quickly that when she cries, she will be tended to (for the sake of this book, we are just talking about normal situations). She learns that she can move her hands and feet and her eyes begin to see objects and shapes. The faces of her parents become familiar and their voices are soothing and comforting.

But humans are designed in God's image, and they are blessed with the gift of language. This gift is a wonder to behold when a child is first learning to associate one word to that particular object. Four-legged furry creature = dog. Four-legged cranky creature = cat. You get the idea.

The gift of language is the ability to communicate at a much higher level. Abstract ideas, complicated theories and deep philosophical discussions result from a shared language. That rectangular object that is always in your hand or back pocket can send messages to someone on the other side of the planet. It's amazing.

But there is a dark side to this wonderful ability to communicate that is so subtle and pervasive that no one can see it (except for your dog).

As soon as a baby learns to associate a word with a person or object, that baby begins to see herself as *separate* from that person or object. When the idea of separation sparks in the infant's brain, it creates a new space to catalog the differences. What makes a cup different than a glass? Why does Mommy smell different than Daddy? You get the idea.

The human brain operates efficiently by recognizing patterns in the trillions of bits of data that it encounters every second. That's the only way the brain can tell if something is a threat or friend – if it recognizes the pattern as dangerous, a chemical reaction happens instantly that will support fight or flight. If it sees the pattern as friendly, there is a totally different reaction.

The cataloging of information by an infant is part of that process of pattern recognition. Bits of data must first be stored before you can recognize a new pattern. The ability to discern between the same or similar patterns only happens when you have already internalized a pattern. This is normal development and necessary.

Dogs learn pattern recognition too. Is that larger animal that puts his head down to eat the grass going to eat me? What about that skinny creature with the long slinky tail that can jump high on a shelf and looks at me with such disdain?

Something else to consider is that dogs and human have the same five senses – vision, hearing, smell, taste and touch. Each has developed and relies on one or two physical senses more than the others. For dogs, smell and hearing are the strongest and most reliable access points to interpret the world. Humans tend to rely mostly on their vision.

Why is this difference important? Because vision is different than eye sight. Vision is what you see when your stories filter the data in front of you. Eye sight is measured by the funny shapes the eye doctor projects on the wall. See the difference (pun intended)?

Dogs see what is in front of them, without stories or filters.

Humans see with their minds, not their eyes.

A crucial difference between dogs and humans is this: we both learn to see with our eyes, but human go one step farther and *learn to see with their minds.*

When you see with your eyes, everyone looking at the object will see the same thing. When you see with your mind, each person's internal filters determine what they see. The object is the same but each person sees it differently.

Humans tell stories about themselves, their place in the world and their value.

Dogs don't.

What do I mean by stories? Stories are what humans tell themselves about a situation, person or thing. You create meaning and add it to a neutral event. When the story about a certain situation or person begins repeating itself to your detriment, then it becomes a limiting story.

Humans create stories around people, situations and themselves that are then used to filter those trillion data bits. Only those data bits that get through the story filter are seen by the human. Every other data bit is excluded.

What does this mean to being able to forgive? EVERYTHING!

Humans give meaning to their world by creating stories about themselves and where they fit in relation to *that* _____ (this is the part where you fill in the blank). If the stories are positive and empowering – great! If, on the other paw, the stories are critical, limiting and judgmental – watch out. The human will only see what supports his story, and he will discount, ignore or be unaware of anything that contradicts or disproves his version. When you add the need to be right to this scenario, there is no room to forgive.

Limiting stories stand at the intersection of righteousness and judgment. Stories based on fear, comparison or lack of worthiness are the crux of your sorrow, pain and depression.

Let me give you an example. A dog will use his extraordinary sense of smell to decide if he should eat the dead bird that just fell from the tree. Depending on the type of dog (hunting v. a purse accessory) he may or may not act on that impulse.

A human will see the same dead bird fall from the tree and start looking around to figure out what just happened. His mind immediately starts asking questions, such as "What killed that bird?" "Did it die and then fall, or did the fall kill it?" and finally, "Is the sky falling?"

The human immediately analyzes the situation, adds layers of meaning to an event that was simply a part of Nature, then concludes (based on fear) that something else may occur.

A dog just decides if he should eat it or not.

The stories that people create about themselves, their lives, their past and their future are what make it necessary to remember forgiveness. Dogs don't create stories, because they always know who they are and why they are here.

> *Dogs know they are love. Dogs know they are here to love a human. That is their divine assignment.*

> *Dogs don't create stories about anything. They are free to forgive everything.*

> *Humans create stories about everything and don't want to give them up. That's why they find it so hard to forgive.*

Combine the talent for story telling with the need to be right and the idea of forgiveness flies right out the window. The need to be right is so powerful that the human clutches his story with a white knuckled grip, stubbornly refusing to let go even when the evidence proves him wrong.

Let me share this story with you to illustrate this point.

A story about stories

One summer afternoon, two boys decided to go down to the river. It had been raining for days and they knew the water would be higher than normal. They wanted to see if their tire swing was any closer to the river.

The boys could hear the water long before they could see it. This was unusual but not alarming. As they walked down the familiar path, they noticed that the tree limbs were heavy with water and the grass that lined the path was bent. The air was heavy with moisture and the birds were just a bit more hushed then normal.

When they arrived at the bank of the river, they couldn't believe it! This was not their normal, placid river that surrounded them in coolness on a hot, summer day. The place where they usually sat and enjoyed the water was no more – instead, it was transformed by the rushing water into an angry, swirling energy of liquid.

The boys looked to their left to check on their swing. It was suspended just above the water, when it should have been 10 feet in the air. As they watched helplessly, the water began to lap at the lower edge of the tire. As the river continued to rise before their eyes, the tire began to become submerged in the angry, rising water.

Jack, the oldest and the leader, gasped and cried, "We can't let the river take it!"

Sam, the younger one and the follower, didn't know what to say. He knew that the river was still be rising and he yelled above the roar, "Jack, it's OK! We'll get another swing!"

Jack was beside himself. That swing meant the world to him, because he and his dad had placed it just so. It was one of Jack's favorite memories of his dad, who had left the family a year before without explanation or notice.

That swing was Jack's only connection to his dad.

Jack jumped in the water and began pulling at the tire with all of his might. The water was stronger than he thought and he could feel it pulling him deeper, toward the middle of the river. He kept pulling on the tire, trying to free it from the rope that was still attached to the tree.

The tire was stuck and so was Jack, convinced that his story was correct that he was willing to risk his life for a tire swing. Sam stood on the bank of the river, shouting at his friend to "Stop!" but Jack was fueled by love for his dad and the loss he felt by his dad leaving.

Sam couldn't believe that Jack would be so stupid to put himself in danger for a dumb tire swing. He had no idea why Jack was struggling so desperately to rescue the tire from the raging water, and all he could do was watch helplessly when the river won.

Just as Jack freed the tire, the river pulled them both into the middle of the raging water. Sam screamed on the bank of the river as Jack clutched the tire, riding the water as he was pulled away.

I shared that story so you could feel Jack's pain at the loss of his dad. His story about the tire and the moments they shared together clouded the reality in front of him. The tire meant more to him than placing himself in a life-threatening situation. All because of the story he created.

The power of forgiveness lies in the willingness to let go of the story and the need to be right. Forgiveness allows a higher purpose to flow into the situation than the muddled and painful existence that results from relying on a story built on false premises. At some point, you have to surrender to something bigger than yourself before you can let go.

Dogs do this in every moment. Watch a dog carefully, and see if she stays stuck in the past or seems worried about the future. It's always about right now.

Great – there's food in my bowl!

Awesome – we are riding in the moving thing and I can hang my head out the window!

Sigh – I love it when I snuggle next to my human.

Time does not exist for dogs, except to satisfy bodily needs. Meal times are important, not because they are set on that round thing with numbers, but because food is essential to life.

Everything else in a dog's world is based on who-he-is: LOVE.

But to humans – time is everything! Rushing out the door because "OMG – I AM LATE!" Being upset in traffic because "I HAVE A MEETING – GET OUT OF MY WAY!" does nothing to carry calm and peace into your day.

Why am I touching on time (which could be a book all by itself)? Because time is part of the story process. Think about it – when you see a doll from your childhood, doesn't it remind you of being a child, playing with that doll? It also may remind you that your brother took the doll away just to hassle you and it made you so angry that you started crying. All of those emotions come flooding into your present moment, because your past story was triggered by an object you call "doll."

You may call this sequence of events a "memory" and that would also be true. But aren't all memories really stories that you cataloged and filed away?

It's when your story memories filter the present moment that the rubber hits the road. If your memory about your brother taking your doll away still lingers even though that was 20 years ago, it's time to forgive him.

It's always time to forgive.

Fear is another reason human create stories. **Stories based on fear are never about the present moment.** They are always focused on past events or future imaginings. Fear stories filter your present moment and blind you to the positive, loving energy that is always present. Instead, you only see the information that supports your story, and you react based on that filtered information.

Forgiveness is the way out of the story maze. When you forgive your past, your present becomes clearer. When you release your fear story and replace it with love, you are confident about your future.

Moment by moment, you create a life built on love.

Dogs know this. It is part of our DNA. It's part of your DNA too, but your stories hide that fact. As a way to remember that you came from Divine Love and so did everyone and everything else, I am sharing a definition of DNA that is another Dogma from the Dog Council:

Dogma

Your DNA is special.

Divine
Nature
Assigned

Start acting like it <3

#HeartDancing   @KathrynEriksen1

When you accept your DNA as **Divine Nature Assigned**, your whole world changes. You begin to think, speak and act as your DNA. You express your DNA because of *what it is* and *who you are in relationship to it.* Authenticity is the norm not the exception and love energy flows through you. Your stories no longer block the energy and you know what to think, do and say in every moment.

Your purpose is guaranteed once you accept your assignment. Your next step is to decide how you want to express it.

Suddenly, your stories are transformed and aligned with a higher calling. Your purpose becomes clear and you are focused on bringing that assignment out to the world. Petty thoughts or needs drop away, because *you have a job to do!* Doubts and fears disappear.

Welcome to my world.

Start clearing up your story filters and see the change in your life. Your relationships will improve, your sense of self will soar and you will be ready to take on the world.

One story at a time.

CHAPTER 3 - STOP CHASING YOUR TAIL (TALE)

Dogs always see in the present moment.

People...not so much. – Avatar

Thank you for staying with me this long. We are almost to the top of the mountain, where you can see into forever. As you climb with me, you are learning how to shed your stories and began to see clearly again. Don't you feel lighter?

After the body's needs are satisfied, why is forgiveness the next level of connection in Doglow's Hierarchy of Connection? It's really very simple – before you can remember your DNA (Divine Nature Assigned), you have to see yourself clearly, honestly and completely.

Your stories add layers to your DNA. When you forgive yourself and others, those stories dissolve and your vision clears. Forgiveness opens the mind to peace.

Humans never understand why dogs chase their tails. Videos regularly circle the internet showing some ding-dong dog chasing his tail, with a human voice in the background urging him faster. Then everyone laughs, including the dog, who is usually grinning at the camera.

Look closely the next time you come across one of these videos. Look closely into the dog's eyes – stop the video so you can actually see into his eyes. You may discover that the dog knew exactly what he was doing and why.

You see with your mind, not your eyes

Dogs live their lives inside a constant stream of now moments. We don't worry or fret about the past or the future. It is only what is in front of us...*right now*...that matters.

Humans tend to create drama around their past and their future, which pollutes the present moment. It's almost as if dogs see each moment as it is presented, clear and pure. Humans see the same moment with story filters that distort, manipulate and disrupt *what is*.

Remember the story about Jack and Sam, the two boys who went down to the river to check on their tire swing? Jack couldn't see the dangerous situation because he was convinced that if he rescued the tire, he would still be loved by his dad. His story colored the moments before him and his decision to get save the tire (and in his mind, save his relationship with his father) endangered his life.

Sam didn't have that story and wasn't emotionally attached to the tire. He could see the danger and knew that the tire was an object that could be retrieved or replaced. He saw the situation much more clearly than his friend and made a different, better decision.

Most humans carry their story filters with them. I have witnessed it time and again – when the actual situation is distorted by the story filter. Instead of seeing what's in front of you, you see through the filter of your story.

#HeartDancing
@KathrynEriksen1

Dogs see with their eyes. Humans see with their minds. That makes all the difference in how they live their lives.

It's like those dark round things you people wear on your nose. The dark lenses stand between you and what you see.

One time, my human put on of those things on my nose! They didn't stay long...but I learned a valuable lesson about the difference between how dogs and humans see the world.

During those few minutes that I looked through the shaded lenses, my world changed. Everything was dark and the shades of grey that I normally use to identify my world were gone. I saw differently – and I didn't like it!

The stories you tell yourself *about* yourself and the world are just like those sunglasses – they shade everything you see and your vision becomes narrowed to the information that is filtered by the sunglasses.

Why is this so important?

Because humans, like dogs, make decisions to act based on what is in front of them. Dogs see what is front of them clearly, since they have no story sunglasses (except when a goofy human decides it would be hilarious to put sunglasses on their dog). Humans wear their story sunglasses 24/7, which means that *what they see in front of them is not what their mind sees.*

Dogs see clearly...in the present moment.

People see through their story filters. They see from their past or future, never in the present moment.

Stories separate you from your Self. When you fill in the gap of information or speculate why someone acted the way they did, it always changes what you see. And suddenly, you are not seeing the situation in front of you. Instead, you see the story that is playing out in your mind.

It doesn't have to be this way. You can learn to see like a dog. My goal is to guide you back to your Self by helping you release your stories.

Instead of telling you about how stories impact what you see, allow me to share an incident that happened to me. Please sit like a good human (O.K. – you can turn around 3 times first) be still and listen.

During one of my lifetimes, I was a seeing eye dog. My girl was called Audrey and we were together for many adventures.

One day, we were standing in the check-out line at the grocery store. Audrey was used to walking the three blocks to the corner market with me and it had become a daily event. Everyone in the store knew us and so did a lot of the customers.

While we were standing in line, the woman who was about to pay became very agitated and angry. Her voice rose to a higher pitch and her words came out in machine gun fashion from her mouth. The cashier, a sweet high school girl named Bella, was trying to calm her down, but it wasn't working.

A whine escaped my throat but Audrey put her hand on my head to reassure me. And that is when we heard it.

The man behind us started grumbling about "People work hard to pay for their food. She's paying with food stamps and she's upset?" Several other people in line began agreeing or nodding their heads.

At the front where all the action was taking place, the store owner/ manager walked over. Mike was a quiet guy, very soft spoken, but he ran his store with a high expectation of his employees. Mike looked at Bella and smiled slightly, letting her know that it was OK. Her posture relaxed a bit and she backed away from the customer so Mike could take over.

After Mike checked that the balance in the lady's account was accurate and told her that she didn't have enough money to pay for her groceries, there was a two second silence. Everyone within 25 feet was waiting to see how she reacted to this news.

It didn't take long. She started screaming obscenities at Mike, Bella and everyone who was within earshot. Her anger was so palpable that the grumblers in line began voicing their opinions.

It quickly turned into one of those ugly situations where no one is listening and everyone is upset.

Audrey just stood there, frozen. I nudged her hand to ask permission to go, and she unclipped my leash, tears glistening in her blue eyes, reflecting her heartbreak.

I wove through the crowd until I reached the angry woman who didn't have enough money to pay for her groceries. I sat down in front of her and whined, waiting for her to acknowledge me. It took a few minutes, and I had to bark sharply, but she finally broke out of her angry tirade against another customer and looked down.

I sat very still, loving her with my eyes. My mouth was closed and I focused on being an open channel for love to pour through me to her. It took several seconds, but I could see the instant that she felt it.

Her entire demeanor changed from anger to shock. The intense emotion that she was drowning in stilled. It wasn't peace but it was an opening for peace.

The woman tried to speak several times, but the words struggled to come out. The mayhem of discord was still swirling around her, but she and I were inside a bubble.

Love protected us and connected us.

She squatted down in front of me and looked me deeply in the eyes. I held her gaze and felt our connection. After a few seconds, she took my face in her hands and kissed me gently on the forehead. Then she stood up – a different person than before.

"Whose dog is this?" She asked the crowd in general.

At first, no one heard her. She asked again, this time in an authoritative tone that captured everyone's attention. Mike, the store manager, stopped in mid-sentence and pointed to Audrey, who looked like she wanted the ground to swallow her whole. The leash in her hand declared her as my owner.

The strident voices of people talking and not listening slowly wound down. Silence filled the space where anger had just lived. Act I was over; now it was time for the climax and resolution.

As the woman slowly turned towards Audrey, everyone felt the energy shift. Bodies moved backwards as the woman moved. When she was standing directly in front of Audrey, the older lady gently took Audrey's hand and asked her to look up.

Audrey slowly raised her head and her eyes looked at the spot where the woman's voice was located.

"Look at me child," the older woman demanded. Audrey smiled slightly and shrugged, her eyes focused on a distant horizon only she could see.

The woman was about to demand attention again, when she realized the situation. She took one more look at Audrey, the leash in her hand, then back at me. My harness clearly said, "Seeing Eye Dog – please do not touch." The woman shook her head and closed her eyes, saying to herself, "Lordy, Lordy."

I enjoyed this part and I was grinning as only a Golden can, teeth showing and mouth wide open. The tip of my tail was swishing back and forth, sweeping the floor with my joy.

The woman straightened her shoulders and took a deep breath to calm herself. She turned to the small group of people and began talking.

"I have a confession to make," she began softly. "I came in this store to build some things for my grandchildren. Only thing is – I didn't have any money, except for these food stamps. I hate using this to feed my family, but some days, it's necessary." She shook her head and said softly, "This was one of those days."

Everyone was shifting uncomfortably because they knew the embarrassing part was coming up. I decided to do my part and began to lean against several people, nudging their hands. They began to stroke my head or pat me as they listened to her story unfolding.

"When I got up here to the cashier's stand to pay," the lady continued, "I wasn't sure if I had enough money on the account. You ever had that worry mister?" She pointed directly to the man who had been standing behind us, grumbling about people not pulling their weight and taking other people's money.

To his credit, the man looked sheepishly at the woman, then nodded his head.

The woman continued. "When this young girl told me what I suspected, I just lost it. I knew what ya'll were thinking. Deadbeat. Poor. Beaten."

She turned to Bella, the high schooler whose second day on the job had taken a turn that she could never have anticipated. "Sweet child, I am so sorry to take my frustration out on you. Please forgive me."

Bella could only nod, her blue eyes bright with tears. They hugged awkwardly across the counter.

The woman turned to the rest of the people who were mesmerized by her. "I forgot to introduce myself – my name is Lydia James. Yes, I am poor in money, but not in spirit." She stopped for a minute to gather her thoughts and leaned over to me and gave me a hug.

"I forgot how rich in spirit I am when I stood here, feeling embarrassed and so small." Lydia looked around very slowly and acknowledged each person. Then she smiled and said, "I hope you will forgive me. It took this sweet dog to remind me that my circumstances are not what define me."

Time seemed to stand still and everyone waited for someone to respond. My impatience at the stubbornness of humans finally got the best of me. I did the only thing I could to move this situation forward so everyone could see it for what it really was – a great lesson.

I started twirling around as if chasing my tail, barking and looking like a crazy lunatic. My antics provided a humorous interlude and everyone started laughing, sharing in my joy. It broke the tension and people came up to Lydia and hugged her, telling her that it was going to be O.K.

The last person to approach her was the grumbly guy who had made such a fuss. He was a large man, hands rough from hard work, nails unclean. His demeanor was completely different from the indignant man who judged Lydia so harshly. Instead, he was humble and respectful.

"Ms. Lydia," he began softly. "I should ask for your forgiveness. I was rude, judgmental and completely out of line."

She stood there looking at him – and smiled. "Well, I guess we both have a lot to learn, don't we?"

He laughed and they hugged. I barked my approval and returned to Audrey, grinning as she clipped the leash back into my harness. I stretched and sighed...just another day at the office.

Why did I share this incident with you? Because it offers several valuable lessons:

- *Everyone has a back story. Release the need to judge because you will never know their entire back story.*
- *Judgment separates you and the other person. Love always connects.*
- *People all have the same needs – food, shelter and connection.*
- *Don't deny someone their need because you don't understand their back story.*
- *Learn to recognize judgment and make a choice for love instead.*

Let's take a moment and see the scene from each person's perspective, their story filters firmly in place.

Lydia James – she was embarrassed and felt small, so she reacted aggressively towards Abby and the other customers to deflect her pain.

Mike – the store manager – he confirmed the facts and reacted to Lydia's anger by trying to convince her that she was wrong. He wanted to retain his authority in front of his customers.

Grumpy man – he was indignant that Lydia was getting a "hand-out" on his hard-earned money. He was really afraid that someday, he too might need to rely on food stamps to feed his family.

Me (the hero) – I reminded Lydia that she was loved beyond all measure, no matter what her present circumstances seemed to tell her.

Can you imagine how the scene would have been played if each person saw the situation clearly, without their story filters? Lydia would have asked to have the balance checked before she tried to buy groceries; Grumpy man would have seen her distress and offered to help. Instead of anger, discord and animosity, generosity would have flowed naturally.

These types of scenes are played out all the time...and most people don't even realize they are seeing through the story in their head...instead of what is in front of their eyes.

Whenever there is judgment or comparison, there is always a story running in the background.

Dogs don't do stories. Our brains don't work that way. Our only story is to *be* love, because that is who we are. Dogs are love...embodied in a 4 legged, wide mouth, tail wagging bundle of joy.

Because dogs are love and we don't create stories, we also don't need to forgive.

That statement may be a bit bold or brash for you to accept immediately, but think about it. Dogs are love, embodied in a shaggy, 4-legged body. Don't believe me?

When was the last time you walked into the room and your dog did **not** greet you as if he hadn't seen you in ages? Silence...

When you walk into the room, your dog acts like he hasn't seen you in forever. Why? Because to him, it has been forever! Living in the moment does that to you.

Each moment is a new experience. Every second is a new heartbeat to express love. Each tick of the clock is a new opportunity to *be love*.

That is the life of a dog. Moment to moment. Living this way creates a happy state of being, because you are not trying to control or change your world.

Instead, you are *being* in the world.

Forgiveness Leads to *Beingness*

The need to forgive to live a happy life is critical. (Not for dogs, of course.) I refer to the 7 billion creatures that walk around on 2 legs with an attitude of superiority.

Have you compared the happiness levels between yourself and your dog lately? I guarantee that your dog is off-the-chart happy, right now, in this moment. Even when sleeping...

Why is that again? Dogs stay in happiness as their normal state, and humans only seem to experience that state of being rarely, if at all.

The funny thing is that dogs don't have a choice about whether we are happy – it's who we are. People...on the other hand...always have a choice. And they seem to consistently choose to be sad, mad, angry, frustrated – instead of *being* happy.

I have shared what I believe is the key difference between the two species – the ability to create stories. Dogs don't do that – and we stay blissfully happy. Humans are story creating machines, and their happiness level is not going to move or change anything.

Go figure.

You see with your mind through the lens of the stories you create about yourself, your value and place in the world. These stories place you in relationship to your past and future, never your present moment. Your stories filter and distort the NOW – the present moment.

When you see the present moment through the lens of your

limiting stories, you will never respond authentically. The layers of meaning that are piled up on this moment of NOW prevent you from *being*. Instead, you see your life through the composite of your stories and you react from that altered view of reality.

And that is why true forgiveness is so important – to clear the past from limiting or fearful choices, to release those decisions and to begin fresh, right here, right now.

Here is another secret that dogs know and humans forget or ignore. Lean closer and look into my eyes so I know you are listening. Closer…

WHAT BRINGS YOU JOY?

Go...do that.

#HeartDancing
@KathrynEriksen1

Do you see the light of love shining in my eyes back to you? Can you feel it as you allow it in? Stay with me and I will share the one thing that will change your life forever.

Your life's purpose is to live as a being of love.

I will let you chew on that for a few minutes…close your eyes and breathe in that message. Tell yourself, "I am a being of love." "I am love." "I am being love."

And we're back.

You know that dogs are love on four legs. What you don't remember is that *you are love on two legs*. Dogs and humans are different in the physical, emotional and mental forms, but maybe not so different spiritually.

Allow me to explain.

Remember the homeless girl at the beginning of this book? She was cold, wet and miserable. But mostly, she was alone. Separated from her family, her friends…but the true cause of her separation was her lost connection to God, the Divine, the Universe.

> *Dogs never lose the connection. People do, because they get so caught up in their stories. They forget their spiritual essence.*

The good news is that your spiritual essence – your **Divine Nature Assigned** – can never be lost or destroyed. It can only be forgotten. Or ignored.

I am here to remind you. So is every other dog who has ever formed a bond with a human. It's our job. It's what we do.

Your DNA is part of who you are. Accept that fact and the rest will fall into place. Struggle against it, resist it or try to control it, and your life will be one of separation, loneliness and frustration.

If you are caught in a vortex of separation and loneliness, it's only temporary. You may feel caught in a maze of mistakes and misfortune, leading nowhere. Darkness may seem to be your new normal and happiness a distant memory. But there is a way out of the maze.

The way out...is to forgive yourself for believing in the separation.

Remember a dog's view on forgiveness? A dog is love in physical form. A walking, barking, tail-wagging being, expressing love. Dogs express their DNA constantly.

Do you?

To express your DNA, **you must *know that you have the light of love inside of you.*** You came from love and someday, you will return to love. While you are here on planet earth, your job is to *be* love. This is the basic point of knowledge from which all else springs.

When you know you are love, that means you are worthy. You are whole, complete, perfect. The essence of you is authentic, real and connected to Divine Source.

How do I know this? I have lived many lifetimes and witnessed many things that people do to each other and themselves. When the human doesn't believe that they are worthy of love, their thoughts, words and actions reflect it. Pain, anger, sadness and separation are always the result. When the person knows that they are love, everything and everyone around them expands.

Is this making sense? Or have you wondered off in your thoughts and you stopped listening to me? **WAKE UP!**

I have another Dogma to share from the Dog Council. This is the crux of life on earth. This is what you have been looking for and never found. This is it.

Dogma

· · · · · · · · · · · · · · · ·

Being love is your authentic nature.

Start acting like it <3

· · · · · · · · · · · · · · · · · ·

#HeartDancing   @KathrynEriksen1

You may be wondering why I use the slanted letters every time the word *"being"* is used. I want to draw your attention to that word, because it holds the key to happiness, bliss and joy. Think of the word *"being"* as:

BEING

Born to Express the Infinite Nature of God

#HEARTDANCING @KATHRYNERIKSEN1

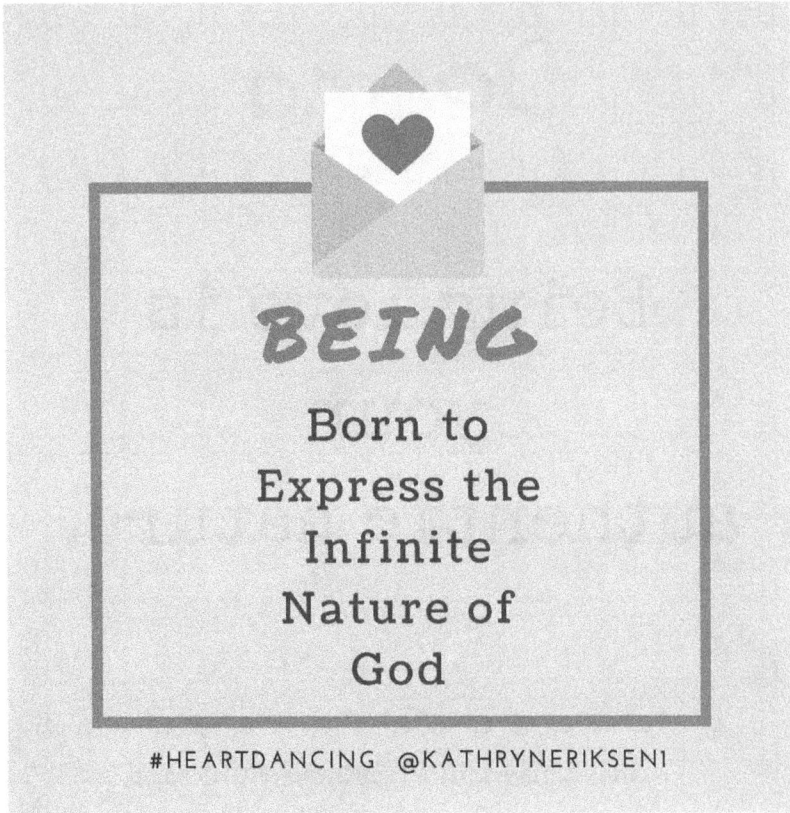

Being love means that you are open to receiving love from your higher source. It also means that you allow that love to flow through you and out into your world.

Dogs allow this flow of love without thought. It's who we are. Humans can also allow the flow of love, but thoughts and the stories that are created stop the flow. That is why humans need to learn how to forgive, so their *being* is clear and love flows in and out with each breath.

Think of it this way. Humans are the only living species that has the word "being" as part of their name. Human B-e-i-n-g.

You never say a "dog being," "tree being," or a "fish being." Why?

Because every creature on the planet knows who they are and what they are supposed to be. There is no choice for a possum to become a squirrel. Or a dog to become a cat (as if that would ever happen ;-)).

Humans are the only species who can create different realities. For example, ten humans can witness the same event, but each one will have a different viewpoint (the story of Lydia and the commotion in the grocery store that I shared earlier is a perfect example).

Dogs are always grounded in their one reality – love. That's why we can forgive so easily.

Humans get so caught up in their created realities (their stories) that they forget they are *beings* of love. Forgiveness is the way back to *being*ness.

Now we are pulling all of the pieces together. Please follow the bouncing ball...

DOGS & HUMANS
both come from
LOVE

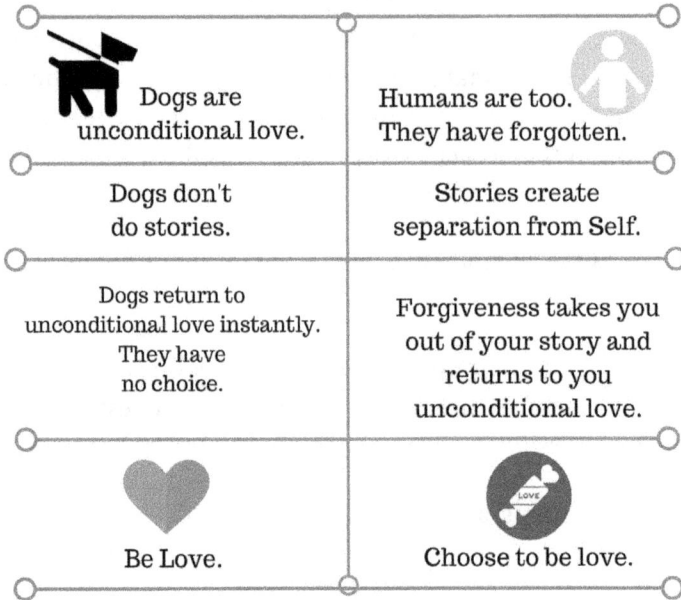

Dogs are unconditional love.	Humans are too. They have forgotten.
Dogs don't do stories.	Stories create separation from Self.
Dogs return to unconditional love instantly. They have no choice.	Forgiveness takes you out of your story and returns to you unconditional love.
Be Love.	Choose to be love.

#HeartDancing   @KathrynEriksen1

Dogs and humans both came from love. This path is shared until…

- Humans learn to talk and label things, people and places as separate from themselves. Soon, you learn to create stories and judge yourself in comparison to others.
- Stories separate and divide, because no one can see your view except for you.
- Forgiveness allows you to take a step back from your story and gain a new perspective.
- When your stories no longer color your view, you are *being* love.

The bottom line is that you cannot express *beingness* when you see life through the lens of your limiting beliefs and stories.

Conflict, judgment and resistance to *what is* are the results of this separation from your Self.

Allow me to show you how to forgive yourself for telling limiting stories. Please take my paw and let's walk down the road of forgiveness together. There may even be a dog bone waiting for us!

CHAPTER 4 - PAWS AND HEEL (PAUSE AND HEAL)

As long as you are breathing, you can forgive. -**Avatar**

Forgiveness is not something that only the Saints or Holy people can accomplish. It is not reserved for only those lucky few who have attended seminary or studied religious texts their entire lives.

Forgiveness is like the air – it is always available in every situation. The capacity to forgive is part of your nature. You are made to forgive…you just don't remember.

Dogs forgive instantly, easily and without thought. A dog's natural state is love and he always returns to that state as quickly as possible. He does it easily, without effort.

Before you were conditioned with stories (which sprang from learning a language), you also knew how to forgive instantly, easily and without thought. Your natural state is love but your stories prevent you from quickly returning to that natural state. Forgiveness is how you get there.

When you can look at your limiting stories with love and compassion and accept that there is a bigger picture than what you perceive, you can transform your stories from fear to love. That is how you begin to forgive yourself. You begin to **shift your stories from fear to love.**

It's almost as if you are also shifting your relationship to that past event that caused you so much pain. Instead of reliving the pain over and over by remembering your fear story, you step outside of that circle and blanket the memory with something greater – love.

Remember, forgiveness never condones what happened. Your forgiveness doesn't say to the abuser, "You're good" or to the criminal, "Not to worry." **Your forgiveness is completely and totally devoted to you, not the other person.**

When you release the fear-based energy that was created by your interpretation of the painful event, you free yourself from being tied to the past. **Forgiveness transforms the energy stored in the aching memory from an anchor to the past to a catalyst for change.** You regain your power to move forward in your life, with greater understanding of yourself and others.

The thought of releasing your old stories may terrify you. "Who will I be without that story?" you might wonder. Trust me whenever you feel that twinge of fear. Go bring your dog next to you (if he isn't there already) and have a quiet moment with him. Look deep into his eyes and ask him that question, "Who will I be without that story?" Breathe deeply and feel your breath come in through your nostrils, fill your lungs and come out again as your chest moves back in. Keep looking into his eyes — do you see the answer? Has it dawned on you yet *who you really are*?

LOVE. You are Love embodied as you.

Dogs decided to join the human pack so we could reflect that truth back to you. God knew that you would need a reminder, so he sent us to do the job. (And based on how humans lavish us with all kinds of silly things – clothes, fancy beds, costumes – we have excelled!)

Dogs know they are Love embodied. Dogs know that each moment is a new opportunity to express that Love.

Humans are stubborn but **you are different**. You have read this far in the book and now you are ready to step into the next grandest version of your magnificent self. The fastest way is to allow all judgmental or critical thoughts to fall away and **let the truth of Love embodied settle in your soul**.

When you finally let that message in and embrace it as your reality – your world view shifts and tilts on a different axis. Compassion and gentleness for yourself and others arise naturally and gratitude flows freely through every moment. Peace and joy become your companions and everyone will comment on your transformation. Just smile and embrace them with all the love you feel. (And don't forget to thank your dog :-)).

That transformation – from fear to love – is why it is so important to pause and heal. You step out of your limiting stories and see them for what they are – something you created to interpret the event or circumstance. There is nothing wrong with you because you decided to judge yourself or make yourself a victim. That's just what humans do. Except now you are about to learn a new way of living in the world, as Love embodied as you.

When you pause and heal, forgiveness is a natural part of that process. Forgiving in the moment is a skill that can be developed, honed and mastered. It is something that dogs and babies do naturally.

You, on the other hand, need some help to remember how it's done. As my gift to you, here are the Forgiveness Steps that are part of the Heart Dance.

Forgiveness Steps in the Heart Dance

Step 1: Recognize your Fear Stories

When you start noticing your limiting stories, look for the underlying reason that you created that story in the first place. Something moved you away from your Self.

When you dig and dig for the first cause of your stories about limitations, at the very core of that set of beliefs is...FEAR. Fear is the motivator, the catalyst, the energy that propels every judgmental thought, word or deed.

Fear of loss. Fear of failure. Fear of rejection. I could go on for the rest of this book, but you get the idea.

Fear is seductive, because it is never about *what is*. Instead, **fear is always based on the past or the future. It is never about the Now.** The present moment is the only place you have to be authentic, loving and accepting of yourself.

Humans avoid fear like the plague. It is painful to be caught in a tsunami of fearful thoughts. The only release seems to be to project it outside. It becomes the story you see when you look at other people who are not like you, who have less (or more) than you, who seem to have it all when you have nothing.

Fear is the first place we visit on our journey to forgive yourself. We are about to enter the Fear Zone.

Take a long, slow deep breath in for 4 seconds. Hold it for 4 seconds. Release in 4 seconds. Hold your breath for 4 seconds.

Now, you are ready to see fear for what it really is. Love in disguise.

FEAR is not something to avoid or project – it is really a sign designed specifically for you to read, acknowledge and consider. It is a gift on your road to a greater version of the grandest vision of your Self.

Think of fear as a billboard:

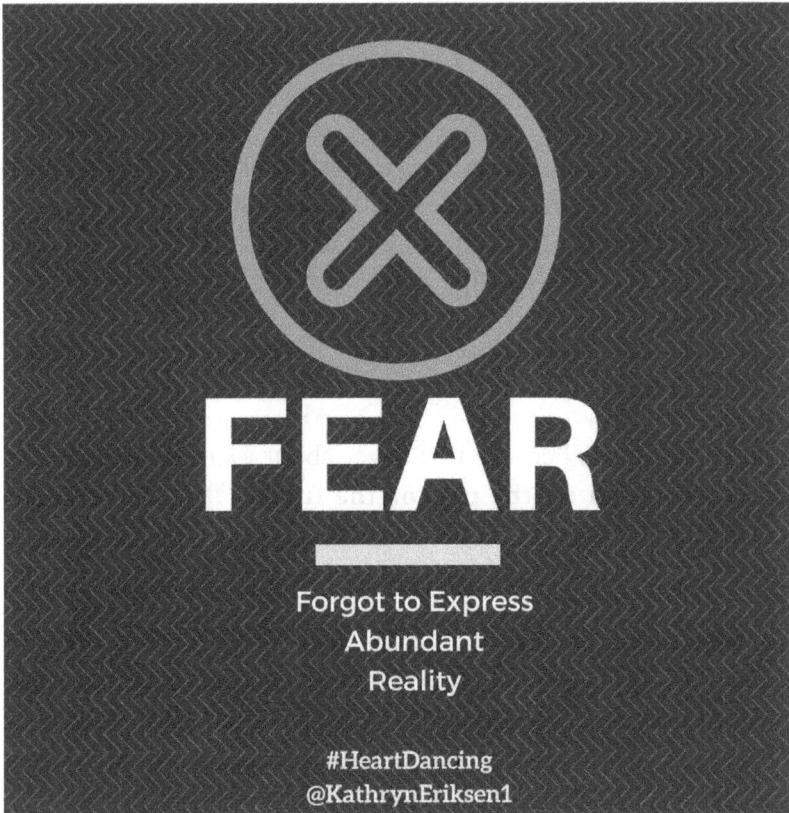

See the tiny letters at the bottom? When you are moving too quickly and just glance at the billboard, all you see are the letters F-E-A-R. Those four letters can easily become a trigger to doubt yourself, devalue yourself and your work and constrict your natural state of happiness.

You have trained yourself to jump into fear whenever you see something that triggers it.

It's like throwing a Frisbee to one of those crazy dogs who love to leap in the air. He can't help himself.

The good news is that when you start to notice that you are chasing the Frisbee of fear, you can make a different choice. You can retrain yourself to not jump when fear is triggered.

How do you recognize your Fear Stories? Your body will tell you instantly when you are in fear. Start to notice when you feel any (or all of the following):

- your muscles tighten (especially your neck and shoulders);
- your breathing becomes shallow or panting (this is the one time you don't want to behave like a dog);
- your thoughts start racing; and
- your heart starts pumping harder.

These physical reactions are signs that you perceive a threat and your body is reacting by going into "fight or flight" mode. The threat doesn't have to be physical. Emotional threats cause the exact same reaction as physical threats. Your body doesn't know the difference.

When you notice that your body is reacting in fear, be thankful. Your physical reaction to what is perceived is the gateway to choosing differently. Your habitual reaction of fearful thoughts can be replaced by a different story!

How can you remember that fear is merely a signpost directing you in a different direction? By giving it a new definition. Fear isn't something to avoid – it is a reminder that you have forgotten your abundant nature.

The billboard on your journey says "FEAR" but when you slow down, you can read the fine print. Take a look again and you will see that "FEAR" is really:

Forgetting to Express Abundant Reality

There is always a moment in time between fear and reaction.

Most people zoom right past fear into their habitual thought pattern, never realizing that they had a choice to take a different exit.

When you feel fear in your body, train yourself to say, "Hi fear. It's you again. Thank you for the reminder." As you are saying this to yourself, take several deep breaths and hold them. Then return to the situation and consider it again.

You will discover that this technique interrupts your habitual thought pattern. You break up the habit and allow yourself time to consider a different response.

You can actually choose to let the Frisbee of fear pass you by. Or not. It is utterly and completely your choice, in every moment, with every breath.

Once you recognize that you have a choice between fear and abundant reality, what's next? This is my favorite part – I get to show you how to use Story Alchemy to transform your fear stories to abundance.

Step 2 – Story Alchemy: Realize You Created the Story

When you create something – a text or email, do you ever go back and correct it? Of course you do – you created those letters to form words, which form sentences that express your intent. As the creator of that message, you are always at liberty to change it (just make sure you do it before you hit "send").

Why is this important? Because you can change or correct the stories through which you see your world.

When you identify a limiting story that is based on fear, you have taken off the sunglasses. You have stepped away from the emotional swirl of the story and now you can observe it to see if it serves you. That why I call this process Story Alchemy, because you have the power to transform your limiting stories.

Dogs don't need to look at their stories – we don't have any!

Remember my girl, Audrey, and the incident at the grocery store? Everyone had a different limiting story about the incident, which caused them to react from their own limited perspective. It wasn't until Lydia took off the limiting story that served as her sunglasses that everyone one else could do the same.

The key is to realize that you are the one who created the limiting story. Yes, YOU. No one else told you how to interpret that event or what meaning to give to it. It's only the person who stares back at you in the mirror…YOU.

The great news is that since you created the story, you can change it!

When you identify a limiting story that is based on fear, you have taken off the sun glasses. You have stepped away from the emotional swirl of the story and now you can observe it to see if it serves you. If you decide that it doesn't serve your highest good, then it's time to move into the next stage of this journey.

Remember, I am your "seeing-eye" dog. Where you are blind, I will lead you. Where you can't see for the story filters, I will show you the way.

And whenever you forget that you created the story that is holding you back, just look deeply into the eyes of your dog. She will remind you that you are a creator!

Step 3 – Story Alchemy: Take Responsibility for Your Stories

This is the critical step. You have moved from believing in your story to observing it. Now you are ready to make the choice to change it to better suit your highest good. Remember about the DNA – Divine Nature Assigned? When you begin to take responsibility for your stories you can choose the meaning that supports your DNA.

When you are faced with a situation that triggers an old story, learning to recognize the trigger is key. It connects you to your creative power. Now that you know your old story was triggered, when you make a different choice you are taking responsibility for your life.

It's always a choice between love and fear. Fear has many disguises (we talked about them in the previous section) but you know it from the way you react. If your shoulders tense, your stomach clenches or your jaw tightens, you are seeing through the lens of fear.

When you contract, it's fear. When you feel expansive, it's love.

When you accept that you have been telling yourself a limiting story based on fear, it's time to pivot. It's time to reframe the story to love.

Step 4 – Story Alchemy: Reframe your Story

Once you realize that you created a limiting story and you want to change it, it's time to look for the gift in the situation.

Wait – I can hear you now. "I had the worst childhood ever. I was sent from one foster family to another. No one wanted me. How can there be a gift in that?"

I know, I know. Your story is the most traumatic, horrific and emotionally debilitating that anyone has ever suffered on the face of the planet. Your story rates a 10 on the scale of crummy childhoods.

It doesn't matter.

Can't you see that you are locking yourself even deeper in your limiting story by claiming that you had it the worst? Your belief that your past is the most traumatic ever experienced by anyone…guarantees that you will not change it. Why would you want to when you are convinced that you win the prize?

Please step down from the podium. You did not just win an Olympic gold medal for the worst life ever lived. It's time to step out of that story and into a new one.

Remember my girl, Audrey? She was not born blind but lost her eyesight when she was about 12 years old. How she responded to that situation goes a long way toward illustrating how to reframe your story.

When my girl Audrey first began going blind, she wept and wailed at the injustice of it. I had not met her yet but she told me all about that dark time. She said as her vision began failing, so did her spirit. She actually thought her life was over.

Audrey was 12 years old at the time, just about to step into womanhood. Her parents tried everything to make the transition easier, but nothing seemed to work. As Audrey slipped into a darker world, she began to withdraw into herself.

One day, Audrey came down to the kitchen to get something to eat. Her mom was sitting at the table listening to a podcast of an interview. Just as Audrey was about to pour a bowl of cereal (she could still see at this point, but not well), the interviewer repeated a quote that sliced right through the walls that Audrey had built to protect herself from more pain.

Audrey's breath caught as she heard the words and felt them rush over her like a waterfall. Her hand froze in mid-air as the new concept embedded itself into her psyche and she sighed deeply, releasing the anger she had held onto so tightly.

The quote that changed her life was by Henry David Thoreau: "It's not what you look at that matters. It's what you see."

It's not what you look at that matters; It's what you see.
Henry David Thoreau

#DroptheLeash
@KathrynEriksen1

Audrey realized in that moment that it didn't matter if she was going blind, she could still see. Her eyesight was only part of the view.

Her heart and soul could see others, know them and share this life experience with them. She could still **see**. And that made all the difference.

Soon, her parents had her signed up for a seeing eye dog and that is when she found moi. ?

The quote that changed her life can also change yours. No matter your situation or circumstance, there is always a different way to see it. That is what the 4th step of Reframing is all about.

Begin to keep track of your limiting stories. Notice when you are triggered. Then go inside your story and see what good has come from it. What did you learn that you would now do differently? Where could you have made a different decision? How could you have loved more?

After you begin to find these limiting stories and reframe them, it will almost become like a game of hide and seek. And you will discover that you have to forgive your past before you can move on.

When you get stuck – play with your dog. Look into his eyes and see the unconditional love and acceptance. That is where you can always return to when you find yourself bogged down in old stories. That place where you are loved and accepted for who you are, not for the decisions you made in the past.

Live in that place where you are whole, healed and loved completely.

As you connect with your dog, you may wonder how we stay in that place 24/7. What is it about dogs that allows us to always turn on the unconditional love energy? There is a very simple answer – Dogs don't need to look at their stories – because we don't have any!

Humans have stories – it's how you give meaning to your world. The key is to know that is what you have done and to reframe those stories that no longer serve you.

The last step in the Forgiveness Process is to release your old story and replace it.

Step 5 – Story Alchemy: Release and Replace

How long have you held on to that old story? Are you like a dog with an old bone – all the flavor gone but it's still clenched in your mouth? Are you refusing to let go?

I have discovered that people hold onto their stories when they believe that their memory of those events is the right one, the correct interpretation, the litmus test of truth. As long as you believe you are remembering the truth, you won't release your very precious, limiting perspective.

It all comes down to whether you are willing to shift, pivot or move slightly. It may be fear that is keeping you in place. You have to decide whether you will stay small inside the fear, or use it as a catapult to move into a new story.

Fear is nothing more than Forgetting to Express Abundant Reality.

Journaling is always helpful at this point. Write down everything that you think could happen if you release your old story. Ask yourself: "Could I survive that?" As you make your way down the list, you will realize that Yes – you can survive that. You will also realize that you have already survived so much and you are still here.

Releasing your old story always involves forgiving yourself.

When you consider your story and why you chose it, also think about how it kept you playing small. Please consider this question: Isn't it time for you to live your life, not the one that is filtered by your limiting stories?

If you answered "Yes," then please, by all means, release the old and replace with the new.

Why keep playing small when there is a wonderful world to explore, learn and grow? Just drop that old story – you are on a mission to create a much larger, grander version of yourself!

Still feeling some resistance to giving up the old story? It does take practice. You are in the habit of telling yourself that old worn out version whenever it gets triggered. It will take focus and commitment to replace the old story with the new one.

At least you are not like the poor elephant, a magnificent animal whose very size and weight is jaw dropping. But if an elephant is tied to a stake when it is young and less strong, it learns to stop trying to break free. Even after the elephant has grown into a huge adult, it will still remain tied to that stake, even though it could easily gain its freedom.

You, my friend, have mental stakes in your thinking that tie you down. You are a Human *Being*, remember? The only species who can dissolve the inner limits and create a new, more empowering reality.

Drop the leash of your limiting stories. Return to Who You Are.
Love.

We have covered a lot of ground, and I would not be a very good teacher if I did not leave you with a summary of the Forgiveness Steps. I know that you are very visual (with your eyes as well as your mind), so I created this nifty graphic to remind you to use the Forgiveness Steps in every moment that you feel constricted or tight.

As you move forward, you will become more proficient in recognizing fear and immediately dropping into the 4 steps of Story Alchemy. And when you forget – go be with your dog. He will remind you by his very presence and love that you have strayed.

He may just pick up his leash…and stand by the door, waiting to play outside. That is your invitation to drop your leash, and be here, now, in the present moment.

FORGIVENESS STEPS

- Recognize Fear
- Realize you created the story
- It's your responsibility
- Reframe your story
- Release and Replace

#HEARTDANCING   @KATHRYNERIKSEN1

CHAPTER 5 - BURY THE BONE

Forgiveness is seeing the light of love in the other person, no matter what they did. – Avatar

Why do dogs bury bones? Why do people clutch their limiting stories as if their life depended on it?

Dogs bury bones because we love to dig, make a mess and save the bone for a later time. That's it – there is no mystery to it. (Finding where the bone was buried could become a bit of a mystery, but that's part of the fun, isn't it?)

Humans have a much harder time releasing their old, painful stories and being here, right now, in the present moment. Hopefully, by using the Forgiveness Steps outlined in the last chapter, you will discover that it is much easier to re-frame your old stories into powerful, supportive narratives. Tiny baby steps are just as valuable as big A-Ha moments. The key is consistency and willingness.

We now turn to the **practical face of forgiveness and what it looks like in the world.**

Now that you know that all human beings share DNA that comes from the same source, you can choose to see the light of love in others. Remind yourself that the other person's behavior is not their true, authentic self. For truly, "they know not what they do."

Keep this definition in mind as we move through real life examples of forgiveness. When we look with the eyes of *being*ness, everything changes.

3 Types of Forgiveness

There are 3 types of forgiveness:

- Forgiveness of self;
- Forgiveness of others; and
- Forgiveness of situations.

Take a walk with me down these 3 paths of forgiveness.

Forgiveness of Self

Forgiving yourself is perhaps the hardest of all. But it is essential to begin with you, because you can never forgive anyone else if you haven't given yourself grace.

This is a quick exercise that you can extend to as many situations as you desire.

Turn to your journal and write down 3 things or situations that you handled poorly. Think about what you did and who it hurt. Allow the emotions to flow but don't get caught in them – that is counter-productive. Instead, just keep listening to the sound of my voice…

Do you have your 3 things? I can wait while you write them down…

Now, for each item, ask yourself if you would have behaved differently, reacted less vehemently or chosen a different action, *if that same situation presented itself to you right now.*

For each item that you answered "Yes" to, write the following statement: "Yes, I would have chosen differently." Sit with that for a moment and feel its truth.

When you are willing to see that you would have behaved differently *if that same situation presented itself to you right now,* then you are ready to forgive yourself.

It's that simple.

The fact is that you can't go back in time and choose differently. No matter how many people you hurt and no matter what consequences followed your past decisions. The past is behind you and no amount of fretting, thrashing or self-abuse will change that simple fact.

It's time to let go of the story that keeps you mired in the past and not living in the present.

Once you are solid in the knowledge that you would have chosen differently, go back and revisit the "How to Forgive" section and use those steps to transform your story. Remember to allow love to flow into your being as you use these processes.

When you start forgiving yourself, you will notice something amazing. Your world will shift and tilt just a bit. As you live each moment in forgiveness, your *beingness* will begin to emerge and you will see with your heart, not your head.

And that makes all the difference.

Forgiveness of Others

When you hold a grudge against someone else, does it really hurt them? They may not even realize that you are angry. Even if you did share your hurt with the other person, you may still not be in your authentic place if they don't apologize or act the way you think they should. They may even not recognize the depth of their transgression.

Have you ever tried to convince someone of how much they hurt you, and they just didn't get it? How much time and energy did you spend making your case, only to have it fall on deaf ears? Why was it so important that you would damage the relationship further?

Because you wanted to be right. To be heard.

Sadly, you can't control other people. You can only control your reaction, your story and your continued efforts to sustain that story.

Please reread the Fake Forgiveness section at the beginning of this book if this does not make sense.

Are you back? Great! So how do you forgive someone who hurt you?

Go back to your journal and write down everything that person did, all of your hurt and frustration, etc. This is not for anyone's eyes but your own. Writing it down helps bring it out in the open, so you can see it more clearly. When it stays inside your mind, the story tends to get garbled and distorted as time passes.

Summarize why you are upset in one sentence. Then go to Byron Katie's website and go through "The Work" process. She is a master at leading people through their thoughts and looking "behind the curtain" to the real issue.

Usually the real issue has something to do with fear. When you identify your fear, remind yourself that fear is really:

FEAR

Forgetting to Express Abundant Reality

#HEARTDANCING   @KATHRYNERIKSEN1

Forgiving others may swing you back around to forgiving yourself. The other person may have triggered an old limiting story in you, causing you to react negatively. If you discover that to be true, rejoice! The other person just helped you identify a limiting story that you can now alchemize ?

Forgiveness of Situations

The final type of forgiveness involves situations or forces beyond anyone's control. Natural disasters come to mind, as well as health issues such as cancer, chronic illness, etc.

When you have been doing your clearing work for a while, forgiving situations will become much easier. You will realize that this is part of your life's journey and you can see it as a growth opportunity, instead of railing against the injustice of it all.

This reminds me of another story about Audrey, the young girl who lost her eyesight when she was a teenager. I became her seeing eye dog.

After Audrey and I settled into a routine, life became easier. We knew each other's breathing patterns, how we slept, ate and had fun. But most of all, we were tuned into the mood of the other.

One day, after I had gone outside to take care of business, I trotted back to Audrey's room. A friend was over visiting and she was talking excitedly about learning to drive. I immediately sensed that Audrey was being polite, but couldn't wait for her friend to leave.

After dinner, Audrey was unusually quiet. I nuzzled up to her and put my head in her lap, waiting for her hand to stroke me like she always did.

Her hand never moved.

I pushed against it, but still...no reaction. Audrey was staring into space, a sad look on her face.

She finally leaned down and hugged me. "Avatar, I never thought about not being able to drive." Her voice dropped and she turned away, lost in her sorrow.

I got off the sofa and walked around to face her. I licked her face to let her know it was going to be O.K. It didn't make a difference and I could see that she was crying softly.

She didn't want to be helped right then, so I laid down next to her feet so she would still know I was there.

Later that night, Audrey's mom asked her about her friend and what they had talked about. Audrey shrugged her shoulders and mumbled something, but I was not about to let her get away with that kind of dismissive teenager response.

I barked, looking at her mom with an expression that said, "There's more to it than that."

Audrey's mom laughed and patted my head. "Avatar, I swear, sometimes I wish you could talk!" I barked again and they both laughed, but it was more of a sad sound that came from Audrey.

The tension eased a bit and Audrey turned to her mom, tears streaming down her face. "I won't ever be able to drive – it's not fair!" she exclaimed. Her mom gathered her in her arms and let her grieve over the loss of this rite of passage.

After some time, her mom hugged her tight and said, "Honey, I know this hurts. You are different than your friends. There will be more things that they can do that you can't."

Audrey sniffled as her mom got up to bring the tissue box over to the bed.

"I don't know why you lost your eyesight," her mom continued. "But I do know that you are just the person to bring light and love to others."

Audrey smiled slightly. Her mom was always telling her that, but now she wondered, "How can I do that when I can't see?"

"It's how you respond to these differences that determines your direction. When you see it with love, you will find a way."

Audrey was silent for several minutes, working through what her mom had just shared. She finally took a deep breath and wiped her nose one last time. She sat up straighter on the bed and turned to her mom while placing her hand on my head.

"I don't know why this happened to me, but I know I can still be someone special." She paused and then said teasingly, "Maybe I will be the first blind teenager to climb Mt. Kilimanjaro!"

They laughed at her statement and hugged again. I jumped up and received my own embrace, while I kissed them both.

Such great advice from a mother who could only sit by and watch her daughter cope with a disability that would knock most people over.

When you find yourself in a situation that seems out of your control, the first step is know that you are going to be O.K. Meditation and deep breathing are great ways to calm yourself. Place reminders such as "I am Love" and "The Universe has my back" in places where you can see them. Your bathroom mirror, your computer screen...create a meme and make it the background image for your phone.

As you move back into a calm and peaceful state, ask yourself these questions:

- Is this true?
- If it is true, what is the worst thing that can happen?
- Can I survive the worst thing?

In Audrey's situation, it was true that she would never be able to drive a car like her friends. The worst thing that could happen is that...she could never drive a car. Could she survive that? Yes, because she was willing to accept the truth in the situation and be herself inside that truth.

After acceptance of the what can't be changed about the situation, you face a pivotal moment of choice. Do you resist what can't be changed or do you acknowledge the truth and decide who you are...inside of that truth?

So much angst and pain is caused from trying to change a situation that you do not control. The only thing you *can* control is your reaction to it. When you use these mindfulness techniques, it returns you to your Self and you can see more clearly.

Never Forget the Kong®

We are almost at the end of our time together. You have been a good human to have shared these words, thoughts and ideas with me. I want to share an idea and an image that will remind you to never, ever stop forgiving.

Have you ever noticed that dogs can be one of the most persistent animals on the face of the planet? One of my favorite toys is the Kong. A dog bone fits inside and it can take me hours to work that sucker out of its plastic housing.

I never give up on a Kong, because I know the treat is inside, waiting for me to devour it.

What is your "Kong"? What makes you get up out of bed in the morning and keep going all day?

Whatever your answer, when that motivation is destroyed (layoff) or suddenly gone (death or divorce), then what? When your motivation springs from things or people *outside* of you, any changes can capsize your boat.

But when your juju, mo-jo, or whatever you want to call it springs from *inside*, nothing can stop you. It's almost as if your essence, your *beingness*…is the sweet spot. And your goal in life is to always live from that place.

Dogs live this way without thinking. Humans think too much and forget about living from the sweet spot.

The Dog Council has given me permission to share another Dogma with you. This one you can print out and tape it anywhere you like where you can see it frequently. It will remind you that life is not a bed of roses and there are thorns that prick you. But it's your job to keep going and never give up.

Dogma

• • • • • • • • • • • • • • • • • •

Life can throw you around.
It can tear you to shreds.
But if you are still breathing and you are able,
your job is to get up and try again.

• • • • • • • • • • • • • • • • • • •

#HeartDancing   @KathrynEriksen1

Never give up on the dog bone of bliss.

To get to that sweet spot where the dog bone is waiting...now that's living!

You may be wondering how you get to that sweet spot. Forgiveness is the open door that you must choose to walk through. Once you make forgiveness a habit, you will discover there is so much more waiting for you.

Bliss. Joy. Peace. Knowing. Acceptance. Love.

You may disagree with me that dogs can feel emotions. Your logical mind may be screaming right now that it's just not possible for dogs to feel. Something undefined in you recognizes that all living beings share the same source energy, but your mind rebels and stomps that knowing into pulp (or tries to).

If you are in that place of struggle between what you know to be true and what your mind demands of you, you are not alone. It is that conflict that leads so many people away from their essence and down the yellow brick road of their humanness.

Now it's time to step into your *beingness*.

Look at your dog the next time he is inside a moment of bliss. Watch him closely and see if he is distracted by anything other than being blissful. He may get interrupted by the doorbell or the cat jumping on the counter, but usually he can return to that blissful state.

Where there is nothing else but that moment.

Dogs never leave their *beingness* – it's who they are. Humans leave it behind and then wonder why they are not happy. Looking outside of themselves, they never find the answer. But when they look inside, there is was all the time.

It's time to look inside.

Listen in Silence

Once you catch a glimpse of your *beingness,* you will want more. But how do you get more when the world demands you look away from the truth of yourself?

Meditation is the single, most powerful way to still the mind. In meditation, your breath is your guide, not your thoughts. The space in-between your thoughts is where your *beingness* is waiting for you to embrace it.

Remember **Doglow's Hierarch of Connection**? He used the word "connection" instead of "needs" because he felt strongly about several key concepts. For the sake of brevity, I will summarize these concepts as they apply to humans:

- You came from a place bigger than you can imagine.
- You are loved unconditionally and wholly.
- Your DNA (Divine Nature Assigned) is an integral part of you.
- You can connect and express your DNA at any time.
- Your *beingness* (Born to Express the Infinite Nature of God) is the expression of your DNA and the reason why you are breathing right now.
- As a human, you have the choice to express your *beingness*. Dogs don't have that choice because they *are* their *beingness*.

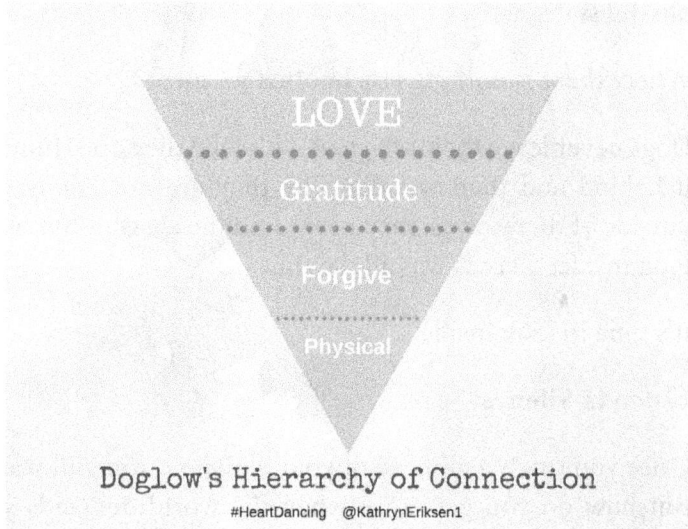

LOVE

Gratitude

Forgive

Physical

Doglow's Hierarchy of Connection

#HeartDancing   @KathrynEriksen1

Doglow created the Hierarchy of Connection to help humans see the layers of perception that are possible when you live from your *beingness*, as a human. Forgiveness opens the door to the other layers of gratitude and love.

Do you understand now why we looked at forgiveness first?

The limiting stories you tell yourself cover these other layers of perception and connection. When you begin to wipe your perception lens clean and see yourself clearly, gratitude and love are the natural consequences.

Our goal is to live with the connection to a greater source of love. To allow that love to flow through you as you move about your day. (That is what a dog does, by the way). To allow the flow of energy to be expressed by you in time and space.

Dogs don't need meditation. People do. So even though I don't meditate per se, I will give you some guidance to get you started. It's what I do.

If you think of meditation as an activity only for monks, sages or weirdos, you have dismissed an ancient practice that is more vital today than when the first "OM" was chanted.

Meditation is a way to still the mind and listen to the heart. Yoga is another process that can accomplish the same thing but for the purposes of this book, we will focus on meditation. (Although I do love the fact that one of yoga's basic poses is the *downward* dog :-)).

As the ancient poet, Rumi, observed, "Silence is God's first language. Everything else is a poor translation."

Meditation is as hard or as easy as you make it. When you sit in silence and allow the thoughts of your mind to float by, it can be disconcerting. Sitting still…doing nothing, is frowned on in our culture. So think of your meditation practice as a time just for you, to soothe yourself, discover new dimensions you never knew existed and to just *BE*.

To BE is the foundation of beingness.

Let that concept settle in for a few seconds. Breathe it in and allow it to settle. Good. Now exhale any negativity that is in your mind. Good. Continue to breath in *beingness* and breath out resistance.

Guess what? You just meditated! (I know that was a sneaky thing to do, but don't you feel calmer, more centered, more aware?)

You are the only one who can experience meditation. No one can do it for you. Words cannot describe the experience you have while in meditation. Books, courses and podcasts can teach the mechanics of meditation, but none of it will help you while the idea of meditation remains in your head. You have to also include your body so your heart can speak in the meditative silence.

You can meditate while you are taking your morning walk or washing the dishes. You can meditate for any length of time (just not while you are driving or operating heavy equipment). Here's a thought – the next time you are waiting at a stop light, instead of checking Facebook, take a deep breath and meditate. It will do wonders for your response the next time someone cuts you off in traffic!

Meditation is a process and a practice. The process can be to sit in silence for a designated length of time, or to listen to a guided meditation. Try different avenues and discover what works best for you. The practice of meditation is how consistently you use it to re-center yourself. Daily is ideal.

When you commit to a daily meditation practice, you will notice a deeper connection with yourself. Habitual reactions will no longer serve you, because you are more present in the moment. When meditation becomes a daily habit, watch and see how you discover your authentic self.

You will discover in your own time that a consistent meditation practice is the foundation of your growth, creativity and ability to stay in the moment. You will no longer fight your monkey mind and clarity of purpose will guide your actions.

How to Get Started

To get you started on a meditation practice, I have included links to several websites, books and guided meditations. This is not a comprehensive list, just a starting place.

Secrets of Meditation, by Davidji

Real Happiness: **The Power of Meditation**, by Sharon Salzberg

10% Happier, by Dan Harris

Science is finally catching up to the idea that meditation is essential to our well-being. On Davidji.com, there is a listing of several research articles and studies that prove the molecular structure of the brain and body changes with meditation.

I can also highly recommend visiting the products page of KathrynEriksen.com for guided meditations that use Story Alchemy questions and techniques to open your perception to greater awareness. A package of five walking meditations is also available.

The best time to meditate is just after you wake up. Your mind has not become active yet and you can reach that place of stillness more quickly.

Meditating in the same place every day also has a powerful impact. Using the same chair, leaning against the headboard of your bed, sitting on the floor on the same mat – routine holds the container for your practice.

It goes without saying that you should be in a quiet room, without interruption or the possibility of disturbance. Your pets may want to play with you (especially if you are on the floor). Dogs are tuned into energy, so try to meditate with your dog and see if he doesn't pick up on the fact that you are being still. If not, put him out of the room until you are done. He will understand :-).

Keeping a journal next to you is also helpful. When you come out of meditation, the insights that may have come to you are worthy of noting in your journal. Think of it this way: You are stepping into a divine space and allowing that energy to communicate. Why not write it down?

These are just some of the suggestions for your practice. As you move forward, you will discover what works best for your lifestyle.

As you learn to live from your *beingness* through meditation, you will discover a sweetness to life. The gentle brush of air on your skin; the colors of a sunrise or sunset; the sound of water being poured into a glass. Physical sensations become more pronounced in your awareness and your spiritual self will rise above your internal horizon.

It's the sweet spot of love.

The place where your heart dances with life.

Life is a dance – your inner world dances with your outer world. When your inner world is in turmoil because of fear, anger, or frustration, it shows up in your outer world. That is how this life is set up to operate.

When you begin clearing and releasing those beliefs and stories that cloud your vision, your outer world begins to reflect those changes. Instead of feeling out of control and chaotic, you begin to accept those things you cannot change and allow divine guidance to be heard.

It's just like a silent whistle that only dogs can hear. **Only you can hear the silent whistle of your Soul** – the Source of Unlimited Love. I can't teach you how to hear it. You were born with that ability, just like dogs were born with the ears to hear that silent whistle.

Isn't it time to listen to the guidance from within?

What's Next?

You have learned why forgiveness is the door to peace. I have shown you how to recognize limiting stories and beliefs and a simple process to change them. This process of recognizing, accepting, reframing and aligning never ends. You know that you can connect to the larger part of you at any time through deep breathing and meditation.

So what's next? (As if all of that wasn't enough for several lifetimes!)

Your path as a human, with a wise dog guiding you, is to BE MORE.

Be more blissful. Be more loving. Be more grateful. You were born to BE MORE.

CHAPTER 6 - IT'S A DOG'S LIFE AFTER ALL

I hope by now that you have a different perspective on forgiveness and its place in your life. As you shift your limiting stories, you will begin to see your life with clarity and focus. As you move into the sweet spot of love and live outward from that place, your life will forever be changed.

When you clear the lens of your perception, your vision naturally focuses on the beauty and majesty that has always been there. When your stories shift from fearful to empowering, you clear the way to become a grander version of yourself.

You are Surrounded by love. You are embraced by love. Be open to giving and receiving love from a greater source.

Forgiveness is the doorway to so much more. So please forgive, forgive, then forgive again. It will lead you to the place that your dog knows best – unconditional love.

Remember the homeless girl in the beginning of this book? I left you hanging about what choice she made when she first saw the miserable, soaked dog waiting outside her makeshift tent. Let's see how that scene played out.

The pounding of the water on the piece of tin that served as her roof was so loud that she missed the soft whining just outside her door. The girl rested with her eyes closed, breathing in the respite of her space. A sharp bark startled her back into the awareness of her situation.

She pulled back the old sheet that served as a shield against a harsh world, and saw a miserable looking dog, sitting patiently in the rain, mouth grinning in greeting, as if to say, "Finally!"

The girl froze for a moment in time, her thoughts and emotions caught in the headlight of the decision that faced her. She had suffered so much pain from the people she loved. Her tolerance level for suffering had been passed long ago, even though she was now living in what many would consider insufferable conditions.

It was the only way to protect herself from more pain.

The girl had lived on the streets for some time. She was used to the hardships, the discomfort, the loneliness. It had become her comfort zone of familiarity and she experienced a strange sense of peace, knowing that no one could touch her heart again.

Until this moment. When another living being waited for her to step outside her comfort zone.

She didn't ask for this! She just wanted to be left alone with her thoughts of the past, her belief that 'she had showed them,' and her pain. She had come to think of her pain as the other person in her life – the only one who understood why she ran away, why she was living life this way.

She even called it a name – Pain.

Pain constantly told her that she was doing the right thing. It calmed her to know that she was not alone, because Pain was always there. Whenever she thought of home or her family, Pain would remind her of the terrible scene with her mother and why she ran away. Pain's monologue kept her separate, alone and unloved.

As she stared at the soaked dog sitting outside of her makeshift shelter, she suddenly saw her life from an outsider's perspective. It was almost as if she was looking down on herself, sitting inside a cardboard home covered with tin, water pouring down from the sky as if tears from heaven were falling.

She saw herself, locked away from any human contact, living a life of hardship. She even saw Pain, sitting beside her, urgently telling her to turn away and drop the sheet so she could stay cocooned inside her small world.

The dog whined again as rain poured off his face in small rivers. As she and the dog locked gazes, she did not see judgment or condemnation. There was no urgency in his gaze, only a patient knowing that something more was waiting for her. Something that had always been there, but she couldn't see it through her pain.

When she finally saw what was always waiting, her heart cracked open and a sliver of light beamed like a flashlight inside her darkness. Her mouth curved in a smile and she laughed quietly.

She finally saw the face of love.

You were once like that girl, choosing to lock yourself inside your pain, refusing to let the light of love shine in your darkness. But now you know the way out. Forgiveness.

You know how to **drop the leash, let go of the past and love in the present moment**.

It's time for you to pull back the curtain on the small world you created to shield yourself from pain. **Let the light of love alchemize your stories and transform them from lead to gold**. As you release the past from your present, your view of the world clears and you see what what always waiting for you.

Love.

Isn't it time to say, "Yes" to love? Isn't it time to step into a bigger, grander, more expansive you?

FORGIVE YOURSELF.
Take yourself off the leash...
and learn how to be YOU again.

#DroptheLeash
@KathrynEriksen1

Love is the song you begin to sing. After you decide to love yourself and see the light of love in others, the natural progression is to step into gratitude. Gratitude is the heartbeat of your life, always supporting you and lifting you higher. As you become more grateful for everything, more love pours in.

You have been a good human, tolerant and obedient. Be willing to chose forgiveness instead of being right. Be willing to see beyond the other person's behavior to their divine light. Be willing to express your *beingness* before your humanness.

As you step into your *beingness*, you give permission for those around you to do the same. And that, my friends, is how DTLers roll.

Remember, when you react from your humanness (instead of respond from your *beingness*), be gentle with yourself. You are reshaping many fundamental beliefs that no longer serve you. That doesn't mean they still won't filter your reality. But now you know the difference and can make the choice that supports everyone involved.

Your life will begin to reflect the changes that have taken place inside. Things that used to trigger you will pass by like a puff of wind. You will no longer be anxious or on edge, because **when you live from your *beingness*, nothing can threaten your safety.**

As you live your life as a *being* encased in human skin, you will discover that your heart leads the way. Your heart knows the direction, action and steps that are in your highest good. The natural byproduct of living from your *beingness* is to be grateful for all that you are.

Forgiving yourself and others releases you. Gratitude pours in and love is not far behind.

When you stand in love, your heart energy connects with those around you. No longer judgmental or critical, your presence in love is felt immediately. Others may not recognize it, but your dog will. And he will celebrate living life in love with you!

It's a never ending cycle. One that you were born to live.

Forgive ➔ Gratitude ➔ Love

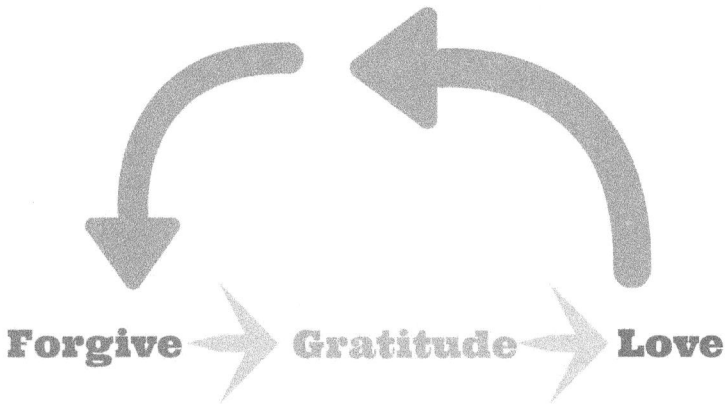

It's a never ending cycle of energy
that continually
flows, expands and gives.

It all starts with forgiveness.
#HeartDancing   @KathrynEriksen1

Gratitude becomes the heartbeat in your life. Love becomes the language of your heart. Together, you begin to dance with something much greater than yourself. Awake and alive, you are now open to receive all of the guidance that has been waiting for you.

As you begin to follow that guidance, you discover that you are now Heart Dancing.

The mantra for Heart Dancers is: Let. Love. Lead. And you know exactly what those three words mean because that is how you live your life. Letting God lead you in the dance of life.

And just think – you learned how to live a magnificent life…
from a d-o-g ;-)! Namaste.

ABOUT THE AUTHOR

Kathryn Eriksen sees the world through a unique combination of logic, sensitivity and spirituality. People frequently ask her, "How did you move from a litigation attorney to spiritual teacher?" She always laughs and admits that, "I desperately needed to learn what I now teach."

Kathryn's work is focused on how to practice the art of **Heart Dancing**, the way to remember your power, harness your energy and dance with life (the practice of Heart Dancing is described in the book by the same title).

You know you have joined the Heart Dancing Tribe when you create and live by your own definition of success. As you begin to live it, your heart will sing and more of what you desire will naturally flow toward you. Your life will begin to feel magical, joyous and authentic, because you are listening to the music of your heart, not the messages from your mind.

If you enjoyed *Drop the Leash*, please tell your friends and share the link across your social media channels.

As a gift to you for reading, sharing and adopting the DTL mantra to "Live from your heart," an excerpt from *Heart Dancing* is included at the end of this book.

Please join the tribe at KathrynEriksen.com. When you share your email address, you receive a free ebook about Story Alchemy, the same process described in this book!

PLEASE JOIN THE DTL PACK

If the story of the homeless girl captured your attention, you may also be curious what happened after she let the dog into her life. **Heart Dancing: A Story Alchemy Adventure** takes place many years later, when Avery, the homeless girl, is now shining the light of love for others to follow. She is never without her companion, teacher and friend. A very special golden retriever named Avatar, who was the voice of this book.

Drop the Leash was created to show the way to living peacefully, joyfully and lovingly. **To stay in touch with other "DTLers," please like the Facebook page**: @DroptheLeashPack.

To stay current on all of the DTL offerings and products, **please join our email list at** KathrynEriksen.com/DTL. Meditations, audio courses and perhaps a live webinar are in the works, based on the concepts in this book. We will dive even deeper into the essence of forgiveness, human v. beingness and living your life from love, just like your dog.

Heart Dancing
on 4 Legs

Love and receive...
like a Dog.

#HeartDancing
@Kathryn Eriksen1

EXCERPT FROM "HEART DANCING: A STORY ALCHEMY ADVENTURE"

Kathryn Eriksen

Just then, Brian came from around the corner to the kitchen. He smiled at the girls and asked Avery, "I couldn't help overhearing your comment about the mailbox. What mailbox are you talking about? And why are the initials so mysterious? Aren't they your initials?"

Avery was rather taken aback at the directness of the question but she quickly recovered. She had reached a decision about the location of her cabin and she knew that letting the Hartt family into her life was more important than maintaining secrecy.

Avery smiled at Brian and explained. "The mailbox is at the end of my driveway. I will have to show it to you sometime." She paused as she considered her next words. Avery turned and looked directly at Brian as she said quietly, "And no, they are not my initials."

She turned around and continued walking, effectively ending the conversation. Savanna's shocked gasp was quickly muffled as they continued toward the deck.

Her father heard it and looked at her, one eyebrow raised to say, "You and I will talk later." Savanna ducked her head and quickly moved in front of her father to avoid any more inquiries about a delicate subject.

As they approached the chairs, Brian turned back to Avery and said with a hint of hurt for being on the outside while everyone else in the group was not. "I would love to see your home. It has obviously been a place that has become important to my wife and daughter." He smiled to soften his words. "What did you study again in California?"

Avery smiled at his tenacity and knew that she made the right decision about no longer hiding her sanctuary. Brian Hartt would never take "no" for an answer and he would have eventually figured out its location. She felt something inside of her shift and expand and knew that she had made the best decision for all concerned.

"I went to California to study at a very special school," she explained as they settled themselves in the deck chairs. Janet and Christine went back into the house to replenish the drinks and food. Savanna could see that her dad wanted to visit with Avery alone, so she followed the others inside.

Brian turned back to Avery to finish their conversation. "What is the name of your school?

"The Avalon School of Divinity."

"Is that a school to learn how to become a preacher?"

She laughed and shook her head. "Not quite." Just then, Avatar stood up and stretched. He wandered back into the house in search of food (and maybe to see if the cat was more hospitable). The break provided Brian an opportunity to consider his next question.

"Then what did you study?"

Avery smiled and acknowledged his curiosity. "Before I can teach others about God, I have to know who I am in relation to God."

"So you studied how to be in a relationship with God?"

"That is a simplistic description, but yes."

Brian decided not to push the point, since he had only met Avery a short while ago. When they knew each other better, they could have a much deeper discussion. He motioned for her to continue her explanation.

Avery was not quite ready to give up so easily. She gazed at the dance of the wind moving through the shimmering aspen leaves, creating beautiful movement. She motioned to the trees and said, "That is how God wants to interact with you."

Brian's puzzled look drew a laugh from Avery. "I just don't get it," he muttered to himself in despair.

"It's O.K to be confused, Brian. You are unlearning all of the rules that have governed your life up to this point."

He turned to her and nodded. "Your mother told me the exact same thing about 30 minutes ago." He took a deep breath and willed himself to relax.

But Avery was not quite finished. She turned back to the sight of the aspen limbs dancing in the sun and said quietly, "Your relationship with God is like a dance – always moving, always creating. Just like the wind moving through those trees."

Brian couldn't help himself. "But I thought that God was constant and encompasses everything."

"He is, but within that constancy are God's relationships. When you were created with the ability to choose – free will – your relationship with God became dynamic."

Brian's legal training kicked into gear. "What do you mean by dynamic?"

"The word dynamic means constant change or motion. So a dynamic relationship with God means that it is always changing or evolving."

Brian shook his head. "I just don't get this spiritual stuff," he muttered to himself. He couldn't help asking the next logical question. "Why would God want to have an ever-changing relationship with me?"

Avery nodded at his persistence and decision to not give up on this line of inquiry. "It's simple. Each one of us reflects God back."

The effect of those words was certainly not simple. Instead, their impact propelled Brian out of his chair and his agitation was obvious. He began pacing back and forth as his mind worked out what Avery just said.

"If we 'reflect God' doesn't that mean that we are also God?"

Avery clapped her hands together in approval. "Well done! And you said you didn't get this 'spiritual stuff.'" Her teasing made Brian smile but his agitated pacing did not stop.

"I can't wrap my head around what you are saying," he admitted.

"That is exactly why I went to school – to learn more about it so I could teach it to others."

Brian nodded and finally sat back down, pausing to take a sip of water. His mind was still working on the puzzle and he finally asked another question.

"How do I reflect God?"

Avery looked deeply into his eyes to gage his sincerity. What she saw made her smile and she continued. "Is it possible for you to see yourself without a mirror or other reflection?"

He thought for a moment and shook his head.

"It is the same way with God."

Brian completed the logical steps. "So God created us so we would reflect God back to God?"

Avery smiled and nodded. She added playfully, "I think of myself as the F.A.C.E. of God." She waited patiently for him to pick up on her message.

"Face?"

She smiled indulgently, loving the feeling of sharing a new concept with a person who had never heard of it before."F.A.C.E."

"I have to ask the question – what do the initials stand for?"

She grinned at the game they were playing. "It's simple, really. Don't make too much of it too soon."

He was not going to be put off. "Does F.A.C.E. have anything to do with the mailbox initials?"

Avery's laughter was contagious. Brian picked up on her joyous energy and started laughing with her, even though he had no idea why. He did feel much lighter and freer from their conversation and he let go of his need to understand everything from a logical viewpoint.

After their laughter died down, he looked at Avery and teasingly said, "Well, just tell me what one of those sets of initials mean."

She smiled indulgently and responded gently, "F.A.C.E. It stands for Feel a Connection Eternal."

Heart Dancing is available on Amazon as a Kindle ebook or paperback.

Join Heart Dancing Tribe, the **secret Facebook Group** for exclusive meditations, challenges and discussions with Kathryn Eriksen, the creator of Heart Dancing. Learn the Art of Being Human.

Heart Dancing
Tribe
The Art of
Being Human